Nurturing the Natural Laws of Peace

NEW EUROPEAN PUBLICATIONS LONDON

This book is dedicated to the future of my family and the future of other families everywhere.

Nurturing the Natural Laws of Peace

through

Regional Peace and Development Programmes

by

Ted Dunn

"Human happiness consists of living in harmony with nature…mutual aid is natural to humankind."
Aristotle

Published in the United Kingdom in 2002 by

New European Publications Limited
14-16 Carroun Road
London SW8 1JT, England

All rights reserved. No part of this publication may be reproduced, stored in a retrieval system, or transmitted, in any form or by any means, electronic, mechanical, photocopying, recording or otherwise, without the prior permission of New European Publications Limited.

This book is sold subject to the condition that it shall not, by way of trade or otherwise, be lent, re-sold, hired out or otherwise circulated without the publisher's prior consent in any form of binding or cover other than that in which it is published and without a similar condition including this condition being imposed upon the subsequent purchaser.

British Library Cataloguing in Publication Data

ISBN   1-872410-25-1

Copyright © 2002 by Ted Dunn

Typeset in Avenir & Minion by www.orbitgraphic.co.uk

Printed and bound in the Great Britain by Antony Rowe, Chippenham, Wiltshire.

Contents

Acknowledgments		ix
Letters of Support		xi
Commendations		xv
Foreword		xvii
1	**Introduction – A Wasted Decade**	**1**
1.2	A Credibility Gap	1
1.3	New Directions	2
1.4	The Cotonou Agreement	3
1.5	The Downside	4
1.6	The UN – A Place Of First or Last Resort?	5
1.7	A Marshall Plan For The Balkans	5
1.8	A Marshall Plan For Colombia	5
1.9	Gorbachev – A Missed Opportunity	5
1.10	Good Intentions Are Not Enough	7
1.11	An Integrated Approach Leading to the Basis of International Law	8
2.	**My Sixty Years Search for the Alternative to War**	**10**
2.1	A Voyage Into The Unknown	11
2.2	Photos from 1942-45	13-16
2.3	Horticulture And Peace Research	17
2.4	Understanding The Alternative to War	20
2.5	Education For Life	23
2.6	Regional Peace And Development	24
2.7	European Affairs	27
2.8	A Realistic Vision.	27

Nurturing the Natural Laws of Peace

3	**Renew and Reform the UN**	29
3.1	The Need For Change.	29
3.2	Collective Security or Collective Insecurity	31
3.3	The UN Charter.	36
3.4	The UN Economic Council.	37
3.5	Finding the Money.	38
3.6	A Marshall Plan and the Rule of Law	39
3.7	Aid	39
3.8	Cancelling Third World Debts	41
3.9	Enlightened Self-interest	41
3.10	Regional and International Law	43
3.11	Importance of Self-Government and the Dangers of Globalisation	44
3.12	Reducing the Bureaucracy in the UN	46

4	**Morality, Justice and the Philosophy of Natural Law**	47
4.1	Introduction.	47
4.2	Understanding Natural Law	48
4.3	Juries and the Rule of Law	52
4.4	Co-operation and the Rule of Law	53
4.5	The Classic Definition of Natural Law	54
4.6	Science and the Rule of Law	55
4.7	Natural Law and the Natural World	57
4.8	The Power of Love, or the Love of Power	59
4.9	Another Definition of Natural Law	60
4.10	God, Wonder, Love and Life Force	61
4.11	The Moral Code	63
4.12	Structures and Dual Citizenship	64
4.13	Codifying, or Legislating for Natural Law	64
4.14	The Growth of Law in the Modern World	66
4.15	The United Nations	66
4.16	World Government and World Governance	67
4.17	The Marshall Plan - Natural Law in Practice	67
4.18	Natural Law in Domestic Affairs	69
4.19	A Specific Proposal for Peace in Regions of Conflict	69
4.20	War is Outmoded	71
4.21	Communications, News, Education and Natural Law	72
4.22	Today the World is at the Cross Roads	73
4.23	Recent Thinking about Natural Law	73

Contents

5	Aid, Conditionality, Self-Sufficiency, Permanency and Globalisation	76
5.1	Harmony of Opposites	76
5.2	Free Trade and Globalisation	78
5.3	Self-sufficiency	81
5.4	A Tobin Tax	82
5.5	National Security based on Co-operation and Education	84
5.6	A Culture of Peace	86
5.7	A Sea or Mind-Set Change in our Perception of Peace Needed	87
5.8	Conditionality and Non-Interference	89
5.9	The Marshall Plan	91
5.10	A Civil Non-Violent Peace Force	93
5.11	Self-Sufficiency and Public Control	93
5.12	Conclusion	94

6	**Education for Life**	**95**
6.1	Race to Hell	95
6.2	Democracy	96
6.3	Changing our Priorities.	97
6.4	Employment	98
6.5	The Voluntary Organisation	98
6.6	Education for Life	99
6.7	The Media.	104
6.8	Values	105
6.9	Paying for Education for Life	105

7	**A Code of Conduct**	**107**

8	**Conclusion**	**111**
8.1	New Thinking	111
8.2	Race Against Time	112
8.3	Hopeful Signs	113
8.4	War is Outmoded	114
8.5	Problems of Today	115
8.6	A Balkan Tragedy or a Window of Opportunity	115
8.7	Preventing Deadly Conflict	116
8.8	Education for Life	116

9	Terrorism - A Postscript to September 11	118
10	Appendix A: The Hague Agenda for Peace and Justice	121
10.1	Root Causes of War/Culture of Peace	121
10.2	International Humanitarian Rights Law and Institutions	122
10.3	Prevention, Resolution and Transformation of Violence	123
10.4	Disarmament and Human Security Agenda	123
11	Appendix B: Marshall Plan	125
12	Appendix C: Film on CD ROM – Peace Through Law	127
13	Index	129

Acknowledgments

This book could not have been written without the support and encouragement in past years of my late wife Bron, and more recently, of many friends, most of whom are Quakers. It has had a long gestation period of about 60 years. These last few years however have also been some of the most valuable and exciting times of my life during which time I have enjoyed long discussions with friends, especially George and Margaret Hicks and Margaret Godden and members of the U3A Discussion Group.

Although the main reason for the book is to offer a practical alternative to war, if it has done nothing else, the search for the alternative to war and violence has enriched my life, and my understanding, in hundreds of ways bound up with the idea of ecology and the meaning and purpose of life. I encourage everyone to undertake a similar journey; if this book will help them on their way it will have served its purpose.

Several names, however, I must thank, in particular, Mary Wong, Dora Apps, Alison Bush, Hilda Taylor, Chris Mort, Rod Usher and Helen Carroll. I am also very grateful for the short letters of support and commendation received, and for the Foreword by The Rt. Hon Lord Peter Archer QC. Not only have all these friends helped in making valuable suggestions about its content, but they have helped enormously in correcting innumerable mistakes. Needless to say the final copy is my own responsibility.

Over many more years I have also been given valuable support by Barbara Panvel and Mervyn Taggart both of whom have consistently encouraged me to continue my research for the underlying basis of international law and the idea of Regional Peace and Development Programmes, the basis of this book.

I must also thank John Coleman, the editor of the valuable journal NEW EUROPEAN, not only for agreeing to publish this book, but also for printing many articles of mine over the years in support of his, (and my), concern for a Europe of Overlapping Circles, an idea that could be emulated in all the other major regions of the world, under UN auspices.

I must also thank John Kay for the cover, illustrating the world being nurtured by two caring hands. Also to Luk Adams for his enthusiasm for converting my video PEACE THROUGH LAW on to CD ROM. Also to Martin Makelroy for assisting and guiding him in this work.

Lastly, for all the help and support given to me by my three sons, Stewart, Alan and Mark, and their wives, Thea, Maja and Mary. At each step of the road they have been involved in one way or another, not least in helping me to lose my fear of the word processor and the Internet.

I must also thank the Oxford University Press for permission to use extracts from THE LAW OF NATIONS and from THE LAWFUL RIGHTS OF MANKIND. Also to Stevens and Sons Ltd for permission to use an extract from LLOYDS INTRODUCTION TO JURISPRUDENCE.

For all this help I am most grateful.

Letters of Support

From **Jonathon Porritt**, *Programme Director of the Forum for the Future*.
I was particularly interested in your chapter 'Morality, Justice and the Philosophy of Natural Law' in the draft copy of the book, *Nurturing the Natural Laws of Peace*. I thought this raised some really important points".

From **Scilla Elworthy**, *Director of the Oxford Research Group*.
In your draft entitled, *Nurturing the Natural Laws of Peace*, you have indeed undertaken useful research covering the whole spectrum of problems facing the planet.

From **Cecil Evans**, *Formerly Assistant General Secretary of Quaker Peace and Service, and a Quaker Representative at the United Nations, New York*.
Ted Dunn's latest book, *Nurturing the Natural Laws of Peace through Regional Peace and Development Programmes* is to be warmly welcomed. It is the logical extension of his earlier works concerned with the need to abolish war through Regional Peace and Development Programmes.

His latest book is fundamentally optimistic about the prospects for abolishing war, provided the requisite political will is demonstrated by governments and civil society to undertake enlightened policies.

These policies would include the use of resources now used for arms for social and economic development in the spirit of the Marshall Plan; and for strengthening the United Nations, making it an even more effective instrument for peace and world order.

From **Bruce Kent,** *Chair, Movement for the Abolition of War.*
Once more Ted Dunn has put us in his debt. There is hardly a page in his new *Nurturing the Natural Laws of Peace through Regional Peace and Development Programmes* that did not make me stop and think.

Everyone with a One World Vision will find it a very useful contribution towards new thinking about global citizenship and the need for regional steps in that direction.

From **George Fairbrother,** *Secretary, World Court Project.*
None of us can live more than one life at a time. As "Peace Activists" we tend to become immersed in specific concerns – the Arms Trade, Nuclear Weapons, UN Renewal – and hardly have time to look over the parapet.

Ted Dunn's publication *Nurturing the Natural Laws of Peace* is therefore welcome. It provides us with a global overview of how human beings can live together at the turn of the millennium, and provides positive solutions to intractable problems.

Natural Justice is the key. It has always been there as an almost unconscious ground for positive law. The idea of public conscience, of our sense of fair play, is almost as instinctive as the propensity for language itself. It is very near to being a defining characteristic of what it is to be human.

Ted explores the history and present-day relevance of this crucial, but elusive concept, and provides an application – Regional Peace and Developments – which is practical and worked out in detail. I commend it to all who are concerned with issues of peace, justice and human survival.

From **Colchester and Coggeshall Society of Friends** *Monthly Meeting. Minute 01.63.*
Ted has spoken to us about the book he is writing. He has worked for peace and peace research for 40 years and has published books and reports of symposia. *Nurturing the Natural Laws of Peace* is now in book form and he hopes to present it to a number of influential people.

We warmly support Ted in this project.

Letters of Support

From **Michael Bartlet,** *Quaker Parliamentary Liaison Secretary.*
Ted Dunn is someone who lets his life speak whether in the Second World War, at work in an isolated Ethiopian hospital or as a market gardener in Essex, he has spent over half a century committed to the causes of justice and peace. Speaking from his pacifist faith, his most recent book *Nurturing the Natural Laws of Peace* is a crie de couer for a more sane and just global society built on the cornerstones of international law and development programmes.

From **Lord Judd,** *Former Parliamentary Under-Secretary for Defence: Former Minister for Overseas Development: Former Minister of State at the Foreign and Commonwealth Office: Former Director of VSO: Former Director of Oxfam.*
In the new millennium we need to understand that real security and peace in its fullest sense are intimately related to justice and responsibility and to economic, social and environmental policy. Migration and its causes is also acutely relevant. It is good to see Ted Dunn addressing this challenge on the basis of his personal experience. He sets an example for us all to follow.

From **Sir Brian Urquhart,** *UN Under Secretary-General for Special Political Affairs from 1974-1986.*
I was interested to see your manuscript and I think your message is a valuable one. A plea for reason, common sense, and enlightened self-interest is important even if only a few people are likely to listen to it. As you rightly say, it is high time to pay less attention to ephemeral sensations and to develop more serious interest in the many promising developments and possibilities for the long-term well being of human society which are now within our reach. In an increasingly fragile overcrowded and vulnerable world it is more important than ever to sustain the right values and to devote the necessary funds and resources to make them a reality. I hope your book gets the attention and success that it deserves.

From **Professor Adam Curle,** *Founding Professor, now Emeritus, of the Department of Peace Studies Bradford University; Professor of Education and Development at Harvard University; Fellow of the American Academy of Arts and Sciences; Gandhi International Peace Award, 2000.*

Nurturing the Natural Laws of Peace

Congratulations on having successfully, indeed brilliantly, completed a volume that represents the summation of your life's dedicated work for peace and development through the means of regional programmes. I hope it brings the fruit it deserves.

From **Gillian Sorenson,** *Assistant Secretary-General of UN External Affairs, New York.*

We have brought your manuscript to the attention of colleagues in the Department of Political Affairs working specifically on issues relating to conflict and peace building. Your initiative in taking on this project and your dedication in bringing it to publication are much appreciated. With best wishes for the success of your work.

From **Richard Seebohm,** *formerly Quaker Representative for the Quaker Council for European Affairs, in Brussels.*

Ted Dunn was ahead of his time in advocating regional groupings as a way to reduce the risk of war between nation-states. He has now brought together the full portfolio of ideas and experience that has made him such a constructive promoter of peace over the years. His new book sets a sense of direction without which our current concern for crisis management will simply lead to more and different crises.

From **Maud Grainger,** *a Student at Bradford University Peace Studies.*
I found your manuscript incredibly interesting and useful.

From **James Lovelock,** *Scientist, who proposed the idea of Gaia-The Living Planet as a "self-regulating" organism.*
Nurturing the Natural Laws of Peace is a splendid statement and its clear and concise way of writing made it a pleasure to read.

From **Tony Benn,** *former Minister of Technology and Minister of Energy.*
Ted Dunn's book is simple, clear and compelling and he brings a deep understanding of the factors that contribute to peace and the dangers which can lead to war. Based on a deep sense of the need for a moral base for society, he makes many practical suggestions, which those in power would do well to consider most carefully. His book is a very constructive guide for those who want to see a just world in a troubled century.

Commendations

SUPPORT GIVEN TO THE IDEA OF REGIONAL PEACE AND DEVELOPMENT PROGRAMMES, AS OUTLINED IN MY TWO EARLIER BOOKS WRITTEN IN 1988 AND 1993.

A serious and thoughtful attempt to deal with what is perhaps the most urgent problem facing mankind.
Lord Peter Archer, QC.

The proposal is an idea which deserves the most serious attention.
H. Dale Anderson, Deputy High Commissioner for Jamaica.

World Peace through Regional Peace and Development Programmes should, for example, wipe out the apartheid system in South Africa.
Ahajd Shehu Awak, Nigerian High Commissioner.

I am a keen proponent of Regional Development. The creation of an International Criminal Tribunal (is) the lynchpin of the future development of international law.
Peter Benenson, founder of Amnesty International.

The concept has very practical possibilities for the Southern Philippines in particular, and in South East Asian region in general.
Nagasura T Madale, Director of the Southern Centre for Peace Studies

I firmly believe the proposal represents a very wise and potentially creative way in which the world could deal with its most pressing needs.
John Sarum, Bishop of Salisbury.

A thoughtful and important document that should be widely discussed.
John Ferguson, Chairman of the United Nations Association and past President of the Selly Oak Colleges.

I think regionalization of the world's problems is the only feasible way.
Johan Galtung, Peace Researcher and founder of the International Peace Research Institute, Oslo.

We here will do all we can to further encourage your idea in Commonwealth capitals whenever opportunities arise.
Christopher Laidlow, when Assistant Director of the Commonwealth Office.

An imaginative and practically oriented work, grounded in a thorough knowledge of the historical record. It is heartily to be recommended.
Shridath Ramphal, Secretary General, Commonwealth Secretariat.

The following is an extract from the Foreword to the book, REGIONAL PEACE AND DEVELOPMENT PROGRAMMES. *I am happy to recommend this essay by Ted Dunn on the changes humanity needs to make in the structure of world co-operation. This co-operation must enable us to solve the great problems of mankind: the problems of security: of poverty,(especially in the underdeveloped countries): of the environment: and of sustainability.*
Jan Tinbergen, Nobel Laureate in Economics. Served as Chairman of the United Nations Committee for Development Planning 1966-1972

All the above commendations are just as important and relevant today, 2002, if not more so.

Ted Dunn.

Foreword

By The Right Honourable The Lord Archer of Sandwell, Q.C.

Is the human race capable of learning? Perhaps the question is too wide and unfocused to admit of an answer. Over the last half-century we have identified problems which were once scarcely noticed. The threat to the environment, and therefore to our own posterity, was the subject of such warnings as Marsh's "Man and Nature", published in 1864, but the need for global action, based on international agreement, was not appreciated before the 1960's.

The dangers of applying escalating technology to war were rarely mentioned before World War Two. The moral responsibility of the affluent nations for those less fortunate became a subject of serious conversation only with the Marshall Plan.

So we are more aware that we are members of one world. Yet protectionism, tyranny, genocide and resort to war are still practised. The techniques to eradicate them exist. What is lacking is recognition of a moral obligation to pay the price. Even those nations who can claim a record free from such practices frequently turn their backs on opportunities to set a better example. Mr Dunn reminds us of the conference in 1990, which I was privileged to chair, on 'A Marshall Plan for Eastern Europe'. We discussed initiatives which, with modest support from the United Kingdom Government, might have spared us, (and more particularly, the victims) many of the subsequent tragedies.

In 1975, Mr. Dunn expounded this theme in his symposium, "Foundations for Peace and Freedom". In "A Step by Step Approach to World Peace", in 1988, he proposed methods of implementing the solution. In this present book he seeks to underpin his previous work by a study of how far practical problems demand a spiritual, or at least an ethical, solution. Are we content to leave too much to the goodwill of national governments? Ethical foreign policies are always to be welcomed, but they are very vulnerable to populist reactions and electoral calculations. Nation states represent people, and perhaps we should work harder on building a culture of peace and justice from the bottom upwards.

His argument will not compel universal agreement. It is possible to support his practical suggestions without necessarily assenting to his understanding of natural law. But is difficult to deny that the problems, which he poses, demand answers, and once again he has placed us all in his debt by initiating the debate.

Lord Peter Archer
House of Lords

*Solicitor-General
in the previous
Labour Government*

1 Introduction – A Wasted Decade.

Ten years ago, after the collapse of Communism and the Warsaw Pact, symbolised by the pulling down of the Berlin Wall, many of us were led to hope that a new era of general disarmament, led by development, would be possible. This change, we thought, would release some of the huge sums spent on defence by the world, to promote social and economic development, security and world law; also as a bonus, give us a Peace Dividend to help finance our own social welfare. Unfortunately, since then the world has had many harsh learning experiences, especially in Vietnam and Afghanistan, teaching us that war can no longer be relied on for imposing peace or righting a wrong, and that alternatives to violence must be found.

1.2 A CREDIBILITY GAP

The UN Millennium Summit of 150 world leaders in New York in September 2000 gave us a glimmer of hope by focusing on concrete development programmes. Many resounding pledges were made at the Summit about improving the lot of humankind, especially the poor, as well as restoring the influence of the UN as the "indispensable common house of the entire human family...and confirmed the UN as the key instrument in settling regional disputes". (*The Independent*, 9 September 2000). Unfortunately there is a credibility gap between pledges and implementation, rhetoric and reality. This book attempts to fill this gap by providing the means, based on the philosophy of Natural Law, as proclaimed by Grotius and many others, to guide us towards the goals outlined in the Millennium Summit. (PS. Please note I am not associated with the Natural Law Party)

1.3 NEW DIRECTIONS

Another positive movement towards peace occurred with the publication of the Final Report of the Carnegie Commission entitled PREVENTING DEADLY CONFLICT and its call for "non-violent solutions". The importance of this well documented book is that it has been thoroughly researched and supports many of the policies that have been consistently called for by the peace movement over the years. In particular the Carnegie Commission calls for more study about "regional arrangements" – an idea that forms the basis of this book.

The UN General Assembly has also called for a decade dedicated to creating a "culture of peace and non-violence". The important Hague Conference of Non-governmental Organisations in 1999 has also issued an important series of proposals (see the Appendix).

THE ORGANIZATION ON SECURITY AND CO-OPERATION (OSCE)

A promising beginning towards these goals was also made when the Paris Charter for a New Europe was signed on 21 November, 1990 by all the prime ministers of Europe, including Eastern Europe, and the US. Then followed in 1992, the Helsinki Follow-Up Meeting where it was decided to rename the **Conference** on Security and Co-operation in Europe (CSCE), to the **Organisation** for Security and Co-operation in Europe (OSCE). By renaming this Organisation the hope was that it will in future be able to act as "a primary instrument for early warning, conflict and crisis management". The need for the OSCE was also seen to be in accordance with Chapter VIII of the UN Charter calling for "Regional Arrangements". Unfortunately, the OSCE was undermined by NATO making almost impossible demands of "take it or leave it" attitude from Prime Minister Milosevic causing him to demand the removal of OSCE observers at a time when they were most urgently needed, a demand that should have been resisted. Both the UN and the OSCE have therefore been bypassed and starved of money and political will and their status and ability to perform their work has consequently been diminished, just at a time when they were most needed. The time has surely come for the resources and political will, at present commanded by NATO, to be redirected to the UN, the OSCE, and the Council of Europe, (Europe's most neglected organisation), especially now that the Warsaw Pact has disintegrated and is no longer a threat. The idea of a new UN, or EC, or OSCE Non-violent Peacekeeping force (as discussed in chapter 3 about Renew and Reform of the UN), must also be supported.

Another hopeful sign was the publications by the US Institute of Peace, an independent non-partisan federal institution created by Congress in 1984 to, 'promote research, education and training in the peaceful management and resolution of international conflicts'. Although I am suspicious of work financed by any government, I have found the publication about 'The OSCE and US Foreign Policy' particularly good and enlightening, especially coming from the US, in its conclusion that,

> 'what is most needed to enhance the role of the OSCE in security affairs is an increase in the commitment by member governments, especially the United States, to work through the OSCE…Above all by placing the emphasis on diagnosis and prevention rather than shows of force to avert war, the OSCE offers the potential to save lives and vital resources that might have been lost as a result of wide-spread violence anywhere on the Eurasian continent.

(Copies are available from the US Institute of Peace, 1200 17th Street NW Washington, DC 20036)

1.4 THE COTONOU AGREEMENT

Another turning point occurred with the signing of the new Lomé Agreement in 1999, now renamed the Cotonou Agreement. This Agreement between the 15 member states of the European Community and the 71 African, Caribbean and Pacific States (the ACP states) makes many splendid recommendations supported by two to three billion ECU's a year over twenty years. The Agreement also supports regional programmes and co-operation with the civil organisations to create a new form of governance for tomorrow. Unfortunately, the **operational machinery** to implement these splendid aspirations is not yet clearly defined and the fear is that the good intentions will be frustrated by bureaucracy and endless conferences (see The Courier – the official magazine of the EC and ACP countries).

1.5 THE DOWNSIDE

In contrast to all these hopeful developments, the reality is that, despite the ending of the Cold War and the dissolution of the Warsaw Pact, the Western World refuses to implement the Agreement made to disarm and redirect resources in accordance with the Final Document of the 1st Special Session on Disarmament of the UN General Assembly, 1978, to use these resources to establish the social, economic, and political basis of international law.

Over the years this failure of governments to act in accordance with their promises has been made worse by the failure of the idea of Globalisation and by many development programmes under the auspices of the IMF and the World Bank (see chapter 5). Fortunately recent changes for the good seem to be taking place in these organisations but whether they will be adequate remains to be seen. Other organisations, such as the UN Development Programme and many of the specialised UN agencies, have been doing good work, but because most aid has usually been given to **individual countries**, without any adequate agreement about the nature of regional or sub-regional co-operation, their work is of limited value. Most aid given has also been tied to narrow capitalist principles of free trade globalisation to the neglect of self-sufficiency, making it almost impossible for the poor countries to compete with the rich countries (see chapter 5).

Past failures to prevent war have also been because our leaders have relied on the idea of deterrence, a policy of bluff that has repeatedly failed from the Ethiopian war in the 1930's to the recent wars in Iraq and Yugoslavia. Instead, we should have been strengthening the institutions of peace, based on the old philosophy of Natural Law by nurturing the Natural Laws of Peace, (as discussed in chapter 4.)

1.6 THE UN – A PLACE OF FIRST OR LAST RESORT?

Despite these failures to prevent war, the belief in war as a means of preserving the peace, NATO remains supreme, even though there was the opportunity to disarm and institute a new world economic order following the collapse of the Warsaw Pact. Now, in 2002, defence expenditure threatens to rise dramatically on the back of The Son of Star Wars. An estimated 63 billion dollars will be wasted that could better be used for regional peace and development programmes. The hopes of implementing the 1973 Disarmament Agreement will also probably be killed by calling it "out of date" and a new arms race begun. If this happens a wonderful opportunity to establish trust and confidence and international law between the nations of the world will be lost. The work and principles of the United Nations and the OSCE, and the rule of international law, will continue to be seen as places of last resort, when they should be the first.

1.7 A MARSHALL PLAN FOR THE BALKANS?

The opportunity for constructive peace-making, in the Balkans, for instance, similar to the Marshall Plan, as proposed by Milan Panic, the one-time Prime Minister of Yugoslavia several years before the crisis, was completely ignored by press and politicians alike. Instead we waited until ethnic conflicts increased and gave rise to ethnic cleansing and the idea of 'humanitarian intervention' imposed by military force – a policy that only reinforced the determination of President Milosevic to remain in power. The UN was ignored and so too was Russia whose influence at that time could have been decisive. So too was the influence of the OSCE. After the bombing had stopped, however, the EC and the OSCE adopted an enlightened attitude and formulated an Economic Development Programme that enabled and encouraged the new Serbian government to send President Milosovic to the International Criminal Court at the Hague.

Fortunately, the idea of a Marshall Plan for the Balkans is still alive thanks to the European Community providing economic aid to reconstruct the region, but no regional integrated gathering of

Balkan leaders has been called to formulate a plan they could call their own. The tragedy is that if only aid had been offered earlier, within a well-conceived regional context, much suffering could have been saved and the foundations laid for other similar regional programmes in Africa and elsewhere. All far more effectively and at much less cost than war. A new vision of peace and security could have been established. Nevertheless much good has been, and still is, being accomplished, not least by the willingness of the new Serbian government to take Prime Minister Milosevic and others to the European Court at the Hague to face charges under the Nuremberg Principles, as discussed in another chapter. Without that aid it is doubtful whether Milosovic could have been arrested. It is a lesson we should learn for Afghanistan and other parts of the world. Unless we have the co-operation of the people, it is almost impossible to arrest terrorists such as Bin Laden and that co-operation depends as much on social and economic human rights as it does on political human rights. In other words peace depends, in the last resort, on winning the hearts and minds of our enemies. There is no other quick fix, especially in today's world of terrorists.

1.8 A MARSHALL PLAN FOR COLOMBIA?

Similar conditions to the Balkans may be seen in Colombia where the US is pouring armaments into the country in the belief that the military can control the drug trade. Instead, we should have supported the plea by Colombia's president Andras Pastrana, made two years earlier, for a Marshall Plan to resolve his country's economic difficulties, the real answer to the drug problem. Clearly we have not yet learnt the lessons of history, that a stitch in time saves nine. The hope must be that the painful lessons being learnt will encourage us to find non-violent alternatives to resolving conflict.

1.9 GORBACHEV – A MISSED OPPORTUNITY.

Another missed opportunity occurred following the disintegration of Russia and the ending of the Cold War. Unfortunately this opportunity (to create a new world order by supporting

Introduction – A Wasted Decade

Gorbachev, with a Marshall Plan for the Soviet Union), was missed. Instead of offering him a life-line, based on generous economic aid and co-operation, we imposed our free market capitalist philosophy on an economy totally unprepared for such a dramatic social, economic and political change. Consequently Russia is now in a state of social and economic disorder and a danger to the world when it could have been enrolled in the cause of peace.

About this critical time I helped to organise a one-day conference for the Conflict Research Society under the title, A MARSHALL PLAN FOR EASTERN EUROPE. If this idea had been adopted as part of a UN world-wide strategy, the tragedies in Yugoslavia, and the unfolding chaos in Africa and elsewhere could have been avoided. More importantly, the status of the Organisation on Security and Co-operation in Europe (OSCE) and the United Nations could have been increased to the point where they would have been in a position to ensure world peace based on social and economic security. But the Peace Dividend and the vision of a Marshall Plan for Russia, and other countries of the world, never materialised and the opportunity was lost.

The last few years have therefore been a painful learning process for all governments. Even the so called "humanitarian wars" in Iraq and Yugoslavia have proved a disaster for the people of these countries, and the storing of hate and fear in the minds and hearts of the Arab world. Surely it would be much better to remove the social and economic causes of conflict by laying down the basis of international law founded on justice and morality **before** conflict occurs (see chapter 4 pages 26-27). Alternatively the potentialities of non-violence, within the context of reconstruction, conciliation and reconciliation programmes after the ending of conflict to reconstruct the region must be supported by a UN Civil Peace Force supported by the non combatant units of the worlds' armies, as outlined in chapter 5 page 18.

1.10 GOOD INTENTIONS ARE NOT ENOUGH

As a member of the UNA I have been constantly impressed by the number of well-meaning conferences dedicated to seeking alternatives to war, but dismayed to find that they invariably result in issuing splendid declarations of intent without the political will and the financial means to implement them. They also lack the vision to create regional structures where all the many aspects of peace may be integrated within well-conceived social, economic and political programmes and Codes of Conduct. Most UN programmes also spawn a vast bureaucracy at Head Office level inhibiting constructive progress at the local level. Instead we need to define the UN's basic principles at the global level, based on the UN Declaration of Social, Economic and Political Human Rights and its subsequent Conventions,(including the ratification of the International Criminal Court) but **implemented** at the regional and sub-regional levels supported by a Code of Conduct. (See chapter 7). But the work of the many UN Specialised Agencies should not be under estimated because without their work the world would be a much poorer place. The World Health Organisation and the Refugee Organisation, for instance, have saved millions of lives. All these agencies have also accumulated a vast range of expertise that must be harnessed for the future.

In view of the above diagnosis this book attempts to bring together some of the main concepts of peace under the law, based on the lessons learned in editing the books FOUNDATIONS OF PEACE AND FREEDOM and ALTERNATIVES TO WAR AND VIOLENCE, as Co-ordinator of the STUDENT PEACE PROJECT, and as a member of the Religious Society of Friends (Quakers). The main lesson learnt is that peace-making and peace-keeping demand a holistic multi-disciplinary approach based on an understanding of Natural Laws, (see chapter 3) and that this task can best, and perhaps only, be undertaken as a co-operative effort, regionally and sub-regionally, within a global context.

1.11 AN INTEGRATED APPROACH LEADING TO THE BASIS OF INTERNATIONAL LAW

With this aim in mind, the following chapters deal with the basis of International Law founded on understanding the nature of God as seen through Natural Laws. Perhaps the most important idea in this book is Gandhi's perception of truth demanding a new philosophy that he calls 'truth force', or Satyagraha, a belief that truth,

Introduction – A Wasted Decade

based on reason, and an understanding about the Nature of God, as seen through Nature, releases a power that can form the basis of international law, without which there can be no peace. In other words we need to discover the basis of a healthy world order where the diseases of the world may be overcome by creating the conditions of health (as discussed in chapter 2). The belief is also held that these ideas, based on diversity and unity, can only be harmonised within a holistic organic whole only possible within regional concepts. Our task therefore is to find and understand the structure, or organisation, to make it all possible, (see chapter 3, Renew and Reform the UN,) for there can be no lasting peace except under the law based on non-violence, conciliation, reconciliation, and above all, co-operation.

Finally, the long-term answer to war must be through education, and this is why Education for Life is included in chapter 6.

2 My Sixty Years Search for the Alternative to War.

This chapter is included to convey why and how my search for the alternative to war began. It is therefore both auto-biographical and political in content.

It all started when I became a Sunday school teacher in a Baptist church in 1937 at the age 18 when the threat of war was a cloud overhanging the world. Gandhi was also in the news with his campaign of civil disobedience and the idea of non-violence and Satyagraha (truth force, see footnote) in India. Preparing lessons with this background made me study the Sermon on the Mount and the relevance of Gandhi's philosophy to my own position, if war was to be declared. The result was that I registered as a conscientious objector and went before a Tribunal claiming complete exemption on moral and political grounds.

The Tribunal however decided otherwise and gave me conditional exemption on the understanding that I joined the Friends Ambulance Unit (FAU), the St John's Ambulance Brigade, or undertook land work. As I was already a member of the St John's, having recently passed their exam, and as I had already applied to join the FAU, this condition presented no real difficulty, but as no opening was available in the FAU I worked on a farm for a couple of months until being invited to join the FAU.

This was another turning point in my life and the equivalent of going to a university. Previously my education was minimal, having left school just before my 15th birthday with the intention of joining the family business. I then went to Liverpool to gain experience in a busy furniture store in a poor part of the city. This experience put me in direct contact with poverty and strengthened my empathy and sympathy for the underdog and underprivileged.

After 6 weeks in an FAU Training Camp in Birmingham I was sent to Gloucester Hospital to undertake all kinds of work, from being a male nurse to working in the kitchen and stoking the boilers. The reason for this move to hospital work by the FAU was because at that time there was a "phoney" war and therefore no demand for ambulances, the battle for Britain being confined primarily to the air.

As the war developed into "all out" war, however, members of the FAU were dispersed to all parts of the world, and I was sent to Ethiopia in response to a request from the Emperor of Ethiopia for forty FAU members to help run the medical services of his country. This was necessary because the Italians, who had occupied and administered the country for several years, were now being deported leaving the country with virtually no medical services outside Addis Ababa.

2.1 A VOYAGE INTO THE UNKNOWN

After an uneventful but fascinating and possibly dangerous voyage from Glasgow via Capetown to Aden in a Dutch cargo ship taking a railway engine and supplies to help the war in Egypt, we eventually reached Aden, from where we continued the rest of the short but eventful journey in a very small Arab Dhocs.

Soon we arrived in Addis Ababa and another important new life opened up before me, but before leaving London I had visited Foyles book shop and armed myself with a small library of medical books, one of which was called EVERYBODY'S GUIDE TO NATURE CURE by Harry Benjamin. This book proved to be invaluable because I was later able to put into practice, in medical terms, the philosophy of Jesus and Gandhi about **overcoming** the diseases of this world with something better than killing – a philosophy that has been with me ever since and influenced my attitude, not only to medicine, but agriculture and international relationships.

After a few weeks of very intensive training in medical work in London and Addis Ababa I was sent to Gimma to help one of the few British army doctors left in Ethiopia. My task was to organise the hospital, but after a couple of months I was recalled to Addis Ababa with the news that I was being sent to a remote, but populous district called Soddu. Armed with a letter from the Ethiopian government authorising me to obtain all I wanted from the well stocked medical stores left by the Italians, and another letter to the Governor of Soddu asking him to give me his support, I left Addis with a lorry load of beds and medical supplies into the unknown.

I need not have worried, however, because the Governor was most helpful and made accommodation available in his house overlooking the town until some dilapidated Italian buildings could be renovated and cleaned. The next two and a half years were to prove the most exciting and valuable time of my life, not only because of the duties involved but because it gave me the confidence to undertake work that previously I would have thought impossible. Starting from scratch with no trained staff and a trickle of patients I was soon confronted with a relative of the Governor with a serious illness. Despite the fact that she died my reputation seemed to soar and towards the end of my stay I was averaging between 200-300 patients a day, mostly comparatively minor ailments, such as conjunctivitis, tropical ulcers, or VD, but some serious. Although I was visited from time to time by a qualified FAU doctor, most of the time I was on my own.

My Sixty Years Search for the Alternative to War

2.2 PHOTOS FROM 1942-45

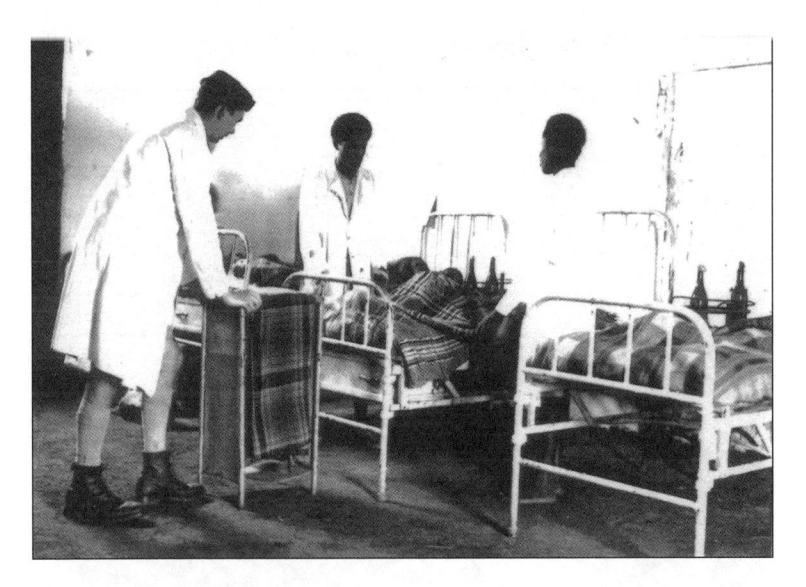

Teaching Bedmaking.

Myself with key hospital staff, with the hospital in the background.

Nurturing the Natural Laws of Peace

This photo interests me because it illustrates the idea of self-sufficiency in an African setting.
I had the house built in a week and the women spinning made her own clothes from locally produced cotton. She also acted as cook for the hospital and the tree being cut down provided wood for the fire to cook the food. I planted several hundred more to compensate around the hospital.

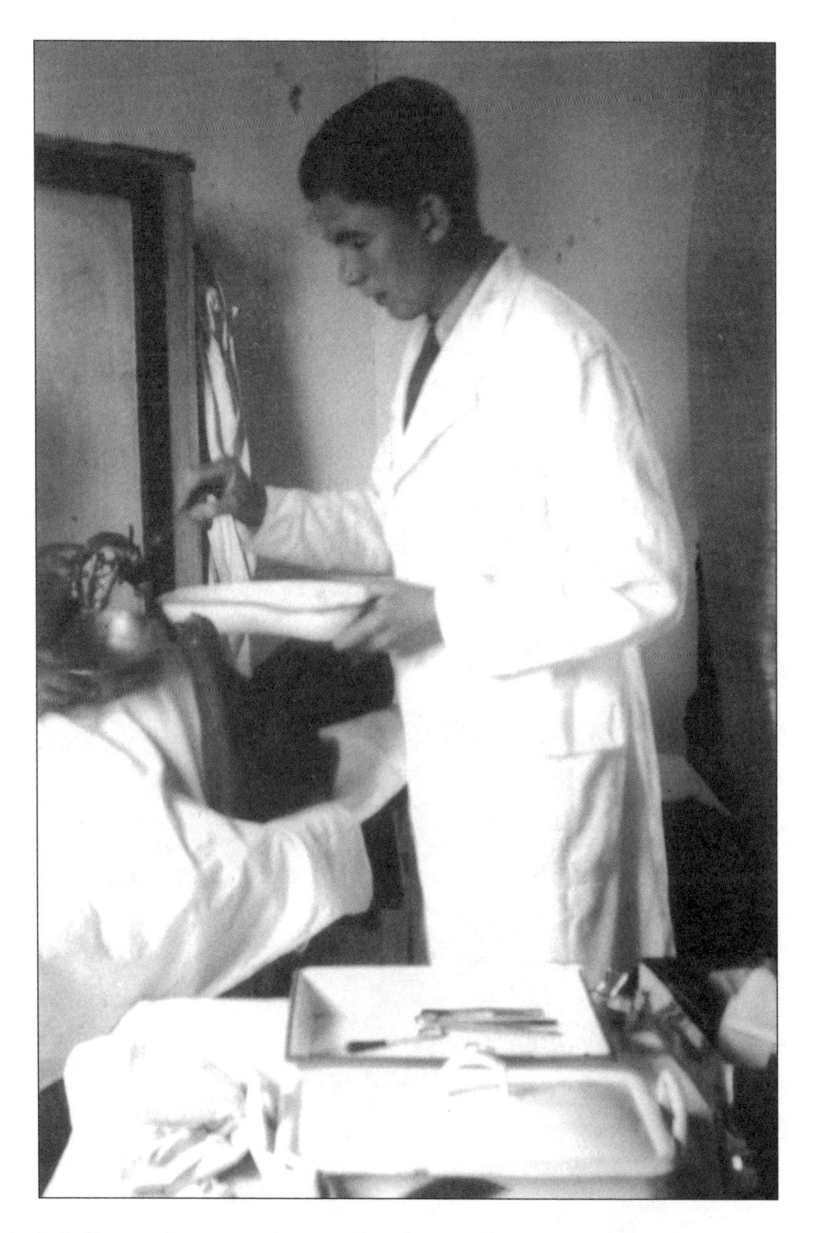

My Sixty Years Search for the Alternative to War

My first major operation – a bomb casualty.

A hand grenade victim with one hand missing, the other being dressed.

Nurturing the Natural Laws of Peace

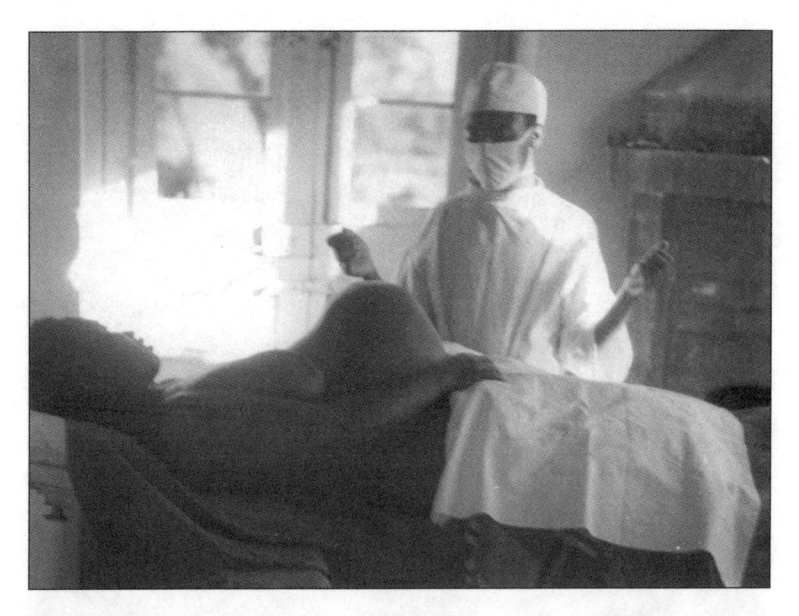

My Caesarean Operation – before...

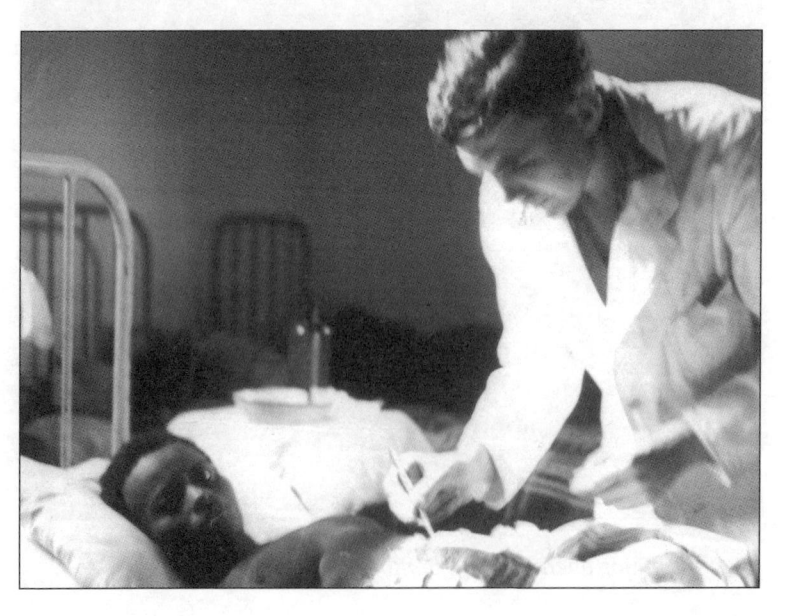

...and after.

With the ending of the war the work of the FAU in Ethiopia unfortunately, and very reluctantly, came to an end, and I returned to London leaving Soddu to its own devices. It was a very sad departure.

2.3 HORTICULTURE AND PEACE RESEARCH

My experiences in Ethiopia was soon to be followed by the decision to accept the offer by one of the Cadbury brothers (of News Chronicle) to develop a small strawberry farm for him near Birmingham where I met my future wife Bron, a Quaker whose faith I also took. Unfortunately Mr Cadbury died before we could develop the farm, but after a few months on another fruit farm, and about a year as manager of a small market garden in Kent, I was accepted as a tenant on one of the Land Settlement Associations (LSA) Estates in Essex where I have remained for more than fifty years.

This period of my life has again been a learning experience in many diverse ways, during which I have been able to combine horticulture with peace research. The LSA itself was also a study of community in action, with about 60 holdings co-operating about marketing, pooling of machinery and the purchasing of goods of all kinds. Even the office work was undertaken as part of the co-operative leaving the tenant the freedom to concentrate on growing crops. It was an invaluable experience about human relationships and was a reflection of the political world in miniature and should be emulated again. Unfortunately Mrs Thatcher put an end to the experiment by selling the estate and now it is only a shadow of its former self. I remain in the same house, however, but without the invaluable help of my wife, who, sadly, died in 1996.

I have always, however, remained faithful in my peace research to my original belief founded on the teachings of Jesus and of Gandhi's concept of non-violence. Although I was an early member of the Soil Association just after the war, and supported the organic movement when Lady Eve Balfour and Sir Albert Howard were pioneering the idea, I was unable to fully adopt their principles because all produce in the LSA was pooled and there was strict pest and disease control. Any flaws in a consignment of produce and everything would be dumped. As with my medical experience in Ethiopia, however, I remained convinced that there is nearly always a much better way of dealing with disease than killing the pest, or disease or artificially feeding the plant directly with fertilisers, **provided** that the organic methods of feeding the soil and nurturing the environment are fully understood. It is not an easy option combining the **art** with the **science** of growing. But given the right conditions the plant, animal, or the body politic can attain immunity from most pests and diseases of this world. This same principle of overcoming the diseases and pests of this world in harmony with Nature's Laws, is, I believe, a universal principle that applies to medicine, politics and international relations. The Natural world has within itself the ability to create a resistance and immunity to the diseases of this world if only we could understand and work in harmony with the Laws of Nature.

In his pioneering book, (AN AGRICULTURAL TESTAMENT, Oxford, p 162), Sir Albert Howard, one of the founders of the organic movement and a civil servant in the Indian government, even maintained that because of his organic methods he was able to maintain a herd of cattle in India free of foot and mouth disease, "even though his cows lived and rubbed noses in a field next to infected cows", a lesson we still have to learn.

Lady Eve Balfour undertook a similar long-term experiment at Haughly in Suffolk but unfortunately, probably because of the long-term nature of the experiment, the vision came to an end for lack of money. The vision remains, however, as is proved by the remarkable growth in recent years of the Soil Association and the Organic movement in general. These long-term experiments, dealing with animals **over several generations**, urgently need repeating today. But the chemical and pharmaceutical industries cannot wait that long and this is the reason why so many wonder drugs such as thalidomide, or pesticides such as DDT, have proved to be long-term disasters and why the public are becoming very suspicious of the claims made by scientists.

The short-term philosophy of the inorganic school is based on feeding the plant directly with artificial fertilisers and consequently killing the life in the soil. Pests and diseases are also sprayed for short-term gain but often with long-term disaster to us all. Instead we should be adopting the philosophy of Jesus to "overcome" the problems of this world with something better, and Gandhi's idea of "non-violence" to all living things. The idealist is gradually being seen as the realist. This is not to deny the wonderful gains that science can bring, but to plead for a fundamental change of philosophy about disease and the direction in which science is taking us. What is wanted is a health service and peace movement, that concentrates more on positive health than disease, and a foreign policy that concentrates on removing the causes of war and promoting the basis of international law. The underlying philosophy affecting all forms of disease in the plant, or animal, or political world, is the same.

On the other hand, scientists, supported by the vast chemical and defence industries are being seen by the public to be leading us to disaster. Remarkable results are being achieved in the short-term but they all too often lead to long-term disaster. Short-termism is the plague of today's world based on and driven by quick profit. The result is that our water is being polluted with nitrogen and other chemicals, the air we breathe is polluted with the fumes of cars and factories, and almost all the food we eat is contaminated with insecticides and fungicides, and grown on soil increasingly devoid of life-giving properties. No wonder many diseases, such as cancer, asthma and depression are increasing. The loss of fish due to pollution and many other environmental problems for short-term gain may soon be presenting us with insoluble problems because of our lack of understanding the Laws of Nature, or because of our greed and demand for short-term results. The number of environmental problems piling up before us is frightening and may not be reversible. To coin a phrase, "you cannot buck nature" because Nature will always have the last word. Usually we do not know the results of our actions until too late. There is even the possibility we may destroy the planet in our ignorance about the germ of 'life'. No one knows what this germ of life is, or where it comes from, and it is as elusive as the idea of God, yet we are playing God in so many fields of science without any clear sense of direction beyond profit.

At the same time the Nature school of thought is starved of money, and the chemical and the arms industries spend billions of pounds on research and the manufacture of weapons of mass destructions. These weapons are so powerful that the world could be destroyed many times over; The truth is, as Jesus said, "no man can serve two masters". Perhaps necessity will soon compel us to recognise the folly of our ways and encourage us to reverse this madness before it is too late.

The same problem faces us in peace research. The arms industry holds the country to ransom demanding Trident nuclear submarines and Eurofighters at vast expense that could be used so much more constructively.

Now the Cold War is over we should be giving aid to the poor countries within well-conceived regional structures (as described in a later chapter) on a scale adequate to remove the causes of war and bring world peace, security and freedom. True, peace research, after many years being seen as disloyal and unpatriotic, is allowed, even encouraged in our universities. International relationships and the idea of citizenship is also being slowly introduced into our schools – but on a scale quite inadequate for the task before us. The peace movement is also too fragile to undertake the huge task before us. For example, the National Peace Council, Britain's major peace organisation has recently been closed for lack of money. It must be resuscitated. Surely it is time for us to reverse our priorities, especially in view of the disasters that are now facing us and because of the misdirection of resources of political will and money. Or are we always to be held to ransom by the militarists and financiers for their selfish ends? Is it that the general public is afraid of change? All this is a far cry from the days when universities were founded as centres for religious studies for the glory of God.

2.4 UNDERSTANDING THE ALTERNATIVES TO WAR

The alternatives to war must depend in future on the power of love, not the love of power, and on recognising that the power of love depends on a **holistic integrated** approach to social and economic justice within a world wide community based on co-operation. The law of love is not some impossible dream but a

My Sixty Years Search for the Alternative to War

realistic understanding about human nature. The soil of our grounding is nurtured based on a sense of generosity, reason and justice and that the spirit of mankind can rise above the evils of this world and generate a new climate based on co-operation at regional, sub-regional and international levels. Conflict can never be abolished but it can be ritualised within courts of law as already happens in many civilised countries and between the countries of Western Europe. But it is war itself that must be outlawed. A beginning has been made by the proposal for an INTERNATIONAL CRIMINAL COURT and the existing EUROPEAN COURTS OF LAW and the many UN agencies.

The need for the alternative to war became very clear to me in the 1960s when the movement was at the height of its popularity. Although I gave CND every support to the movement then, I argued that unless CND could provide a clear alternative to war and undertake a programme of peace research it would fail. The response I had from letters in the press, CND meetings and calling for peace research at CND meetings was disappointing, but with the support of the Bishop of Colchester and local Quakers, the Fellowship of Reconciliation and local CND members we organised a very successful one day conference in Colchester called, A SEARCH FOR THE ALTERNATIVE TO WAR AND VIOLENCE.

The success of this conference led me to believe that a book on the subject was urgently needed and therefore, in 1963, several years before peace research became established, a symposium of 24 essays by many eminent people was published, but without the help of a small local group of supporters, and the advice and support by nationally known peace activists the book would have been impossible. Sir Stephen King-Hall (a well-known broadcaster at the time), said of ALTERNATIVES that, "if some intelligent benefactor donated £1,000,000 (at 1963 prices) to set up a Peace Research Institute, this book would be number one in the Library". The success of this book led me several years later to edit another similar book called, THE FOUNDATIONS OF PEACE AND FREEDOM. This work won the WORLD EDUCATIONAL AWARD in 1976 as, "the book that made the greatest contribution towards promoting the social purposes of education".

Nurturing the Natural Laws of Peace

Two subjects in particular caught my attention and were to play an important role in my future. The first, written by Dr D.V. Cowen, a Professor of Law in Capetown during the Apartheid period about Natural Law, and the second by Peter Manniche about Education for Life. These two chapters seem to me to be fundamental to all peace work and I have developed these ideas further in later chapters of this book. Dr E F Schumacher also wrote a chapter called THE ECONOMICS OF PERMANENCE anticipating his famous book; SMALL IS BEAUTIFUL and Sean Macbride wrote a chapter about HUMAN RIGHTS AND THE RULE OF LAW. It is invidious of me, however, to single out these chapters because the reality is that peace is a multi-disciplinary and ecological concept and what affects the part affects the whole, because, as John Donne says,

> "No man is an island entire of itself; every man is a piece of the Continent, a part of the main; if a clod be washed away by the sea, Europe is the less…any mans' death diminishes me, because I am involved in Mankind; and therefore never send to know for whom the bell tolls. It tolls for thee."

I feel I have been particularly fortunate to edit the above books, and later of have the opportunity to act as the Co-ordinator for a Student Peace Project because all this work has given me a perspective involving the whole spectrum of human relationships, such as anthropology, religion, history, psychology, delinquency, politics, international law, economics, non-violent resistance, animal behaviour, art, to name but a few of the many subjects covered in the above books. I cannot claim to be the master of any of these studies but my hope is that I have been able to gather the essentials of each in my search for the alternatives to war and relate them to the whole. My fear is that future peace research may not fully appreciate the importance of seeing the problems of peace as an integrated holistic concept and therefore unable to find a structure of organisation capable of embracing all these many disciplines. Specialisation is certainly necessary but there must also be the vision to see its place in the whole.

The success of ALTERNATIVES TO WAR AND VIOLENCE and FOUNDATIONS OF PEACE AND FREEDOM later led me to produce a 16mm film called PEACE THROUGH LAW for an American World Amateur Competition. Several years later the film was transferred, with music added, to video. In this film the ideas of Natural Law and an International Criminal Court were illustrated by the use of a garden, an orchestra, and the Court at The Hague. The film also advocated, and anticipated by several years, the idea of self-determination for Wales and Scotland (see appendix for more details).

2.5 EDUCATION FOR LIFE

But Education for Life still maintained a hold on my imagination and, therefore, hoping to combine my horticultural work with the idea of a Peace Study Centre, my wife and I bought a 7 acre holding in Suffolk and for many years we worked towards the vision of a "do it yourself" peace centre where all the facilities for living would be provided but where participants would be responsible for themselves and their studies. Many weekends were organised in this way with the Peace Pledge Union, the Quakers and others. Progress, however, was slow and eventually we decided that we needed planning permission in order to appeal for money to develop. This request was refused by the local authorities, but not before the BBC interviewed me on the 6 O'clock news on Armistice day with a film about the Centre. Not only was permission refused but I was told to stop all peace activities. This was a bitter blow but the eventual sale of the holding enabled us to purchase our present LSA house and land and later retire from horticulture.

Retirement however was only partial because I soon initiated a STUDENT PEACE PROJECT with financial help from the Rowntree Charitable Trust. This Project ran for many years encouraging students who were undertaking a project or dissertation at school or university to relate there work to peaceful relationships by offering them small grants. Sponsors included Professor Adam Curle and Professor James O'Connell, both Principals and Professors from the new Department of Peace Studies at Bradford University. Dozens of fascinating essays were submitted on a wide range of subjects, and once again this work proved an invaluable learning experience. I was helped in the task of assessment by many Quaker friends at Colchester Meeting and by outside experts such as Sir Peter Pears, who, when I was presented with a musical score, offered his advice. In all my life I have been indebted to so many people (especially my wife, family, local friends and Quakers) and for those who are experts in their particular subject in other parts of Britain. Without their support, little could have been accomplished.

As the grant from Rowntree's began to be exhausted I felt it time to close the Project. The small balance remaining was therefore transferred to the Conflict Research Society to enable it to continue making small awards to students undertaking peace research.

About this time I became a founder member of the Christian Action (Colchester Quaker) Housing Association and was its first chairman until it became more firmly established. Although this work was not directly a peace activity, the Association has now established itself as the major charity in Colchester for helping the homeless and unsupported mothers.

2.6 REGIONAL PEACE AND DEVELOPMENT PROGRAMMES

For the last 10 years I have been preoccupied with the idea of REGIONAL PEACE AND DEVELOPMENT PROGRAMMES. This concept originally grew from the recognition that what was wanted was a new structure of organisation, or reform of the UN, capable of integrating all the many aspects of peace, as outlined in ALTERNATIVES TO WAR AND VIOLENCE, and FOUNDATIONS OF PEACE AND FREEDOM, within a holistic concept. This task is almost impossible on a global scale but eminently possible on a regional, or sub-regional level.

I therefore found myself writing many letters and articles to the press, including several for the NEW EUROPEAN journal, (whose policy was, and still is, to support the idea of a EUROPE OF OVERLAPPING CIRCLES.) In other words a Europe from the Atlantic to the Urals of several small regions all co-operating with the EC in the Council of Europe and the Organisation for Security and Co-operation (OSCE) "as a primary aim for early warning, conflict prevention and crisis management". The article I wrote for this journal was called REGIONALISM AND WORLD PEACE, and it subsequently appeared in the same issue as a contribution from Margaret Thatcher! The dialogue about the future of Europe continues in THE NEW EUROPEAN and is one of the most important issues facing us today.

It was about this time that Mikhail Gorbachev was revolutionising the Soviet Union and offering new hope for world disarmament and world peace, appealing at the same time to the West for help and co-operation. As a great believer that "there is" (as Shakespeare says in Julius Caesar) "a tide in the affairs of men, which, taken at the flood, leads on to fortune", I encouraged the Conflict Research Society to arrange a one day London Conference under the title of A MARSHALL PLAN FOR EASTERN EUROPE. This conference was a sell out with many people being unable to get a place. Unfortunately its success did not influence the government, and the window of opportunity to radically change the course of world history was lost, and Gorbachev was banished from power and the hopes that he gave us vanished. What a missed opportunity!

Encouraged by the idea of Regional Peace and Development as an idea within the UN I wrote a booklet, in co-operation with William Apps, called WORLD PEACE THROUGH REGIONAL PEACE AND DEVELOPMENT PROGRAMMES. A second edition was printed later. The success of these booklets soon led me to write a longer work called, A STEP BY STEP APPROACH TO WORLD PEACE-REGION BY REGION. (See supporting letters in the Appendix).

The importance of the Regional idea is that economic security and regional programmes can be initiated quickly, needing only the political will of the United Nations, the EC, or the Commonwealth, to find the money to provide the incentive for the states in any region or sub-region (in Africa for instance) to co-operate. The Marshall Plan that encouraged Western Europe to co-operate and create the longest period of peace and prosperity Europe has ever known provides a good example, illustrating the speed with which a regional plan can be initiated and implemented. It also led to European states (after 100 years of war culminating in the First Great War and Second World War) sacrificing a remarkable degree of sovereignty to regional courts of law. Why, I ask, cannot this example of generosity and vision be initiated by the United Nations for many other regions, or sub-regions, such as the Balkans and Afghanistan, in the world today to resolve their problems?

2.7 EUROPEAN AFFAIRS

A hopeful beginning has been made by Prime Minister Tony Blair and Chris Patten (the EC Commissioner External Affairs for Eastern Europe) in speeches calling for a Marshall Plan for the Balkans. Whether the £30 billion estimated to be needed to undertake the task of reconstruction and development **after** the war will ever be found is doubtful because only about £3 billion has been initially allocated. Nor is Patten's plan a truly regional plan as envisaged under the Marshall Plan unless it seeks involve the whole region **as one concept** including Serbia **as a co-operative effort**. The West should also be encouraging Vladimir Putin, Russia's new President to be involved as the only person with the necessary influence in the region.

£3 billion is of course much better than nothing and still a generous sum but how more worth while and cost effective if this sum of money could have been offered **before** the war, as proposed by Milan Panic, the one time Yugoslavian prime minister from 1992 to 1993. We could easily have afforded the cost if we had the right priorities, because the Cold War had ended and the Berlin wall had come down, so the excuse of an enemy was no longer valid. Unfortunately, the Peace Dividend never materialised and hundreds of billions of pounds continue to be spent annually by the world's rich, and poor countries on armaments, in the false belief that they will bring peace and security. The US is even talking about a new National Anti-Missile Defence system, at enormous cost, which would be far better spent from security and economic points of view, on promoting Regional Peace and Development Programmes. If this policy is implemented we can probably say goodbye to all our hopes of financing the UN to enable it to undertake constructive peacemaking, and probably goodbye to co-operation with Russia and China over disarmament. Let us hope that the enlightened minority in the US will be able to change US policy, or that the technical feasibility of the missile project will prove impossible to implement.

The policy of so-called "defence" has so obviously failed with more people being killed in the last fifty years than in all history. The wars in Russian war in Afghanistan, and the US war in Vietnam and elsewhere have also demonstrated that war is now outmoded and unable to achieve its objectives of peace and security. If only a fraction of the money squandered on those wars could have been devoted to removing the social and economic causes of war through well-conceived regional structures, similar to the Marshall Plan, not only would the causes of war be removed, but the basis of regional and international law would be established on a permanent footing. It has happened in Europe, it could happen in other regions in a step-by-step, region by region, approach to world peace.

2.8 A REALISTIC VISION.

Fundamentally what is needed is recognition that there is a better way of maintaining our peace with security founded on the rule of law and enlightened self-interest, and the principles of non-violence and Satyagraha. It is not an impossible dream as Europe has demonstrated over the past fifty years following the Marshall Plan, but it needs a change of heart and a sense of generosity similar to that provided by the US after the Second World War. Perhaps necessity will force us to change direction in accordance with the saying by Jean Monnet, the founder of the EC, that "people will only accept change when they are faced with necessity, and only recognise necessity when crisis is upon them." Let us hope that people recognise that this crisis is upon us **now** and make the changes necessary before it is too late. Or, to use two more well known sayings, "necessity is the mother of invention", and "a stitch in time saves nine". The financial aid structure of the UN must also be reformed to enable it to undertake this task – region by region as and where possible. Surely it is only common sense?

NOTES.

The Indian word, "Satyagraha", a word much loved by Gandhi is defined by Joan V Bondurant in her book, GANDHI – HIS RELEVANCE FOR OUR TIMES, as, "the constructive transforming of relationships in a manner which not only effects a change of policy but also assures the reconstructing of the situation that led to conflict".

ALTERNATIVES TO WAR AND VIOLENCE is now out of print but copies of the second edition of FOUNDATIONS OF PEACE AND FREEDOM, in paper back, with a Foreword by Lord Caradon are still available at the original 1997 price of £4.50, 400 pages post free direct from the author. A bargain at today's prices!

The booklet REGIONAL PEACE AND DEVELOPMENT PROGRAMMES (44 pages) is also available at the reduced price of £2 post-free. So too is the book, A STEP BY STEP APPROACH TO WORLD PEACE-REGION BY REGION at £4.95, 119 pages post free from the editor, Ted Dunn, 77, Hungerdown Lane, Lawford, Manningtree, Essex. GB CO11 2LX. Tel 0044 (0)1206 230 434.

3 Renew and Reform the UN.

3.1 THE NEED FOR CHANGE.

Because of the UN's many failures to maintain peace and overcome major problems such as poverty and bureaucracy, many people, including those in government and the UN, recognise that the UN is urgently in need of being renewed and reformed.

These are legitimate grounds for change but I suggest the success or failure of the UN depends largely on the support it receives from its member states and the public. The UN Secretary-General can give, and has given, a lead, but he cannot command and is constantly being ignored and over-ruled.

For instance, the previous Secretary-General of the UN, Boutros Boutros-Ghali has written two splendid books called, AGENDA FOR PEACE, and AGENDA FOR DEVELOPMENT, each containing many proposals about peace-making, peace-keeping, peace-building, co-operation and regional arrangements, and, most importantly, about financing the UN. His successor, Secretary General Kofi Annan, has also been pleading for UN reform and has made many valuable proposals.

A working group composed of more than thirty of the most important international names, such as Jimmy Carter, Willy Brandt, Edward Heath and Vaclav Havel, has also contributed to a Report called GLOBAL SECURITY AND GOVERNANCE, containing many important and valuable ideas. There are seven chapters dealing with: 'Conflict prevention'; 'Against Complacency'; 'When Prevention Fails'; 'Operational Prevention'; 'Structural Prevention'; 'Preventing Deadly Conflict'; 'Responsibility of States'; 'Leaders and

Civil Society'; 'The Responsibility of the United Nations and Regional Arrangements'; and 'Towards a Culture of Prevention'.

THE COTONOU ACP-EC PARTNERSHIP AGREEMENT

Another source of hope comes from the new EC-African, Caribbean and Pacific States Partnership signed on 23 June 2000. This Agreement, (now called the Cotonou ACP-EC Agreement), is built on the old Lomé Agreement that expired in 1999. Although not part of the United Nations, nevertheless it directly concerns 71 African, Caribbean and Pacific States and provides a good working model which the UN could emulate. Under the Agreement 15 billion Euros have been allocated over the next 20 years. The Agreement sets out several important priority areas about: trade, regional integration, micro economics, health, education, transport, food security, institutional capacity building, conflict prevention management and resolution, and good governance, all very good proposals backed up with some hard cash in grant form. Special emphasis is also placed on co-operation with the Civil Societies and putting more responsibility on local decentralised democracy. These challenges are acknowledged but they still require (according to a programme spokesperson in the Courier, the official ACP-EC Magazine), "effective implementation, consistent application and reinforced partnership". The money allocated is also probably inadequate for the huge task involved and far less than the aid given to Europe under the Marshall Plan.

The full Partnership Agreement, however, goes to great lengths to detail how the Agreement will be implemented; so much so that I fear it may become bogged down in bureaucracy and argument and therefore lose much of its impact. Too much importance is probably attached to imposing conditions when it would be better to provide more incentives to cooperate. The Agreement may also appear to accord too much importance to being part of a globalised free trade concept and too little to developing self-sufficiency for the rural farmer who forms the overwhelming proportion of the African and Caribbean population. Regional development is also to be encouraged but unfortunately most of the money will be given "to **each** (my emphasis) of the ACP States" and only 1.3 Billion

Euros (out of the total of 15 Billion) to encourage cooperation within Regional Development concepts, the most valuable part of the Agreement. Regional co-operation by the very nature of co-operation would ensure the aims of the Agreement to resolve conflict, encourage management resolution, good governance and reduce poverty. Regional programmes would also be more easily verified. (For more information see the ACP-EU Courier Special Cotonou Agreement and the magazine, the Courier, from the European Commission, 200 rue de la Loi, 1049 Brussels, Belgium).

My fear is that when too many individual countries are involved the problems multiply and co-operation between states becomes more difficult. The same problem, (of resolving world peace through giving aid to individual countries) within a single global context is similar to that now facing the UN. Under the Cotonou Agreement, however, a beginning is being made to encourage regional and sub-regional co-operation.

Whether the good intentions of the Agreement will be implemented remains to be seen because the money involved will have to be spread very thinly to cover the 71 ACP countries over a 20 year period. A process of disarmament should also be included in the Agreement because, without disarmament and a process of regional conflict resolution, the Third World's wealth will be wasted in argument and the ACP-EC agreement consequently undermined. My fear is that the effectiveness of the Agreement will also be undermined by the time and money spent discussing the conditions. (A simplified Code of Conduct for the regions is offered in the Appendix).

Nevertheless the Cotonou Agreement appears to be a real attempt to resolve the major problems facing Africa, the Caribbean and the Pacific countries within an integrated holistic concept and must be commended.

3.2 COLLECTIVE SECURITY OR COLLECTIVE INSECURITY.

There is obviously no shortage of proposals about what must be done at the international level, but why are they so often ignored at the UN? Why cannot we generate the political will to find adequate money to make them really effective? And perhaps more importantly, why cannot we find the structure of organisation to put them into effect?

Here I come to the main stumbling block enshrined in Chapter 7 of the UN Charter where it declares that the Security Council has the power to;

> "take such action by air, sea, or land forces as may be necessary to maintain or restore international peace and security".

These few words, which usually go undisputed and are seen as the corner stone of the UN, must be tacitly ignored and forgotten, or better still discarded, because instead of being the foundation upon which peace can be established, they have proved to be divisive and probably the main cause of collective **insecurity**. From the days of the Ethiopian war when Mussolini invaded that country, to the Korean, Vietnam and Afghanistan wars, and about 100 smaller wars, more people have been killed than in all history. Until this reliance on war (which is contrary to Chapter 1 of the Purposes and Principles of the UN) as a means of settling disputes is (at least tacitly) discarded by the UN, I fear there will not be the political will, or the financial resources, to implement all the many valuable suggestions being proposed. We cannot go in two opposite directions at one and the same time; instead we should be putting more emphasis on positive peacekeeping, peacemaking and peace building, and this determination should be reflected in the financial aid we give to the UN and the political will so urgently necessary. Much good work has already been done by the UN as can be judged by the number of UN agencies, but the funds given are too little and the structure of organisation to co-ordinate the work is inadequate. Well-conceived regional programmes based on good governance, and social, economic and political human rights, together with a UN non-violent Peacekeeping Force now under urgent consideration at the UN and by many Non-Governmental Organisations, as an integral part of the UN, could be the answer.

If reliance on the idea of collective **military** security has failed so conspicuously during the past few years, consuming vast sums of money and killing many millions in the process, what is the alternative? I suggest it must rest on the idea of collective **Economic and Social Co-operation** as outlined in Chapter 9 of the UN Charter, in the belief that if countries co-operate, economically and socially, many of the causes of conflict will be removed and the basis of international law created. The idea of Natural Law and international law, based on non-violent principles, is more likely to become the normal way of conducting international affairs, as discussed at greater length in the chapter about MORALITY, JUSTICE AND THE PHILOSOPHY OF NATURAL LAW.

NON-VIOLENT PRINCIPLES.

Ways of conducting international affairs based on non-violent principles were recognised in 1997 by the prestigious Carnegie Commission, in its important Report PREVENTING DEADLY CONFLICT in which it considers;

> "ways in which international organisations might contribute towards developing an effective international system of **non-violent problem solving**"(my emphasis).

The chairman of the Carnegie Commission, Cyrus R.Vance, US Secretary of State 1977-80, and most of the other members of the Commission all held important positions in governments. Clearly the climate of opinion is changing in government circles from one of outright opposition to anything containing the word "peace", to one that recognises its importance and indispensability. Only a few years ago the word "peace" was outlawed and regarded as a "dirty" word. Today the realisation is growing that there is no alternative. Peace, non-violence and the rule of law are the only ways of establishing our security.

GUIDELINES FOR THE FUTURE.

Fortunately, most of the UN Charter is devoted to co-operation, development and international law and has given us the vision and guidelines for the future. More recently the idea of raising the status of the UN Social and Economic Council to equal that of the UN Security Council has been proposed by the Commission on

Global Governance chaired by Ingvar Carlsson, former Prime Minister of Sweden, and Shridath Ramphal, former Secretary-General of the Commonwealth.

The ideas put forward by the New Economic Foundation; Saferworld; and University of Bradford Department of Peace Studies, The Hague Conference, and many other peace organisations such as the World Development Movement, the United Nations Association, Renew UN, and The World Court Project, are also making valuable and constructive peace proposals, but the one common factor missing in most of these is the need for them to be integrated and implemented within well-conceived REGIONAL and SUB-REGIONAL structures.

WILLIAM BLAKE AND THE PATCHWORK QUILT.

An article in Development Dialogue (an international peace research journal published by the Dag Hammarskjold Foundation) entitled WILLIAM BLAKE AND THE QUILTING BEE, expresses the above theory well by describing the history of the Quilting Bee in Canada where each person was responsible for his or her own patch which in the end came together to form a remarkable whole. The author, Roy Mooney, draws the lesson by saying that:

> "the solutions to the world problems be they environmental or political, can only come through a patchwork quilt. Each piece must have its own integrity. In the end, of course, it is sewn together – as surely as the earth is round, this is happily unavoidable. But there is no quilt unless each patch is complete".

Mooney then adds that William Blake in 'Jerusalem', said it more eloquently:

> "He who would do good to another must do so in Minute Particulars; General Good is the plea of the scoundrel, hypocrite and flatterer."

The UN is often guilty of speaking in general terms. For instance, the Millennium Summit 2000 at the UN, initiated by the Secretary General, urged the Heads of State or governments to take action in many areas. All very splendid aspirations but unless they are **implemented in "minute particulars"** they will remain, like so many past resolutions at the UN, liable (such as the Treaty on the Non-proliferation of Nuclear Weapons) to the accusation of being hypocritical statements.

There is no excuse for this state of affairs because the UN Charter in Chapter VIII gives the Organisation the authority to encourage specific regional development programmes. This chapter in the UN Charter is of special importance because it gives the UN the opportunity to provide a structure of organisation enabling it to integrate, through co-operation, all the many aspects of peace and security through regional, sub-regional and local organisations within a holistic and ecological concept not otherwise possible on a global scale. Everything must depend on the integrity of each individual stitch if the whole is to succeed, but each stitch must comply with the vision of the whole.

Nor will co-operation between ethnic communities, or between states, be encouraged if aid is given to **individual** countries, which then promptly use that aid to buy more armaments in order to wage war more effectively against its neighbours, or spend it on some other extravagance. Regional aid, given to assist the "minute particulars" such as appropriate sustainable development programmes, could avoid this misuse of **aid** and be implemented quickly. The Marshall Plan was conceived and implemented within a matter of months and showed what can be done once there is the political will; but it must be done within a Code of Conduct as discussed in chapter 7.

The failure by the UN to create this 'patchwork quilt' is probably one of the main reasons why so many people feel "aid fatigue" and why the political will to provide aid on the scale needed is so sorely lacking. It is essential therefore to formulate agreements about the **principles** governing international law at the global level, but to **implement** them locally and regionally. In the expectation that when they are put into effect, through well-conceived regional development programmes, regional law based on natural justice will follow as a logical consequence. So much aid in the past has been seen to have been wasted because the causes of war and poverty have not been dealt with and because there have been no well-conceived regional structures to provide the incentive to co-operate.

3.3 THE UN CHARTER.

It is worth recalling that Paragraph 3 of the UN Charter under the heading REGIONAL ARRANGEMENTS says:

> The Security Council **shall** (my emphasis) encourage the development of pacific settlement of local disputes through such regional agencies, either on the initiative of the states concerned or by reference to the Security Council.

Paragraph 3 therefore gives us the encouragement and authorisation to build a new structure of organisation, and a new World Order fully in accord with the Charter of the UN.

Regional Peace and Development Programmes must use this authorisation and opportunity to encourage regional development by offering those regions in desperate need generous aid on the understanding that they agree to co-operate within well-conceived CODES OF CONDUCT based on Principles already agreed at the important Prime Ministers' conferences over the past decade.

Subjects discussed at these conferences included:
The Environment, the Habitat, Human Rights, Woman's' Rights, and Social Development.

These Agreements, although not binding, provide important guidelines for the future and should therefore be incorporated within regional programmes. They are due to be renegotiated and strengthened in the future months and years and should be widely supported. The Hague Conference, about the Environment, attended by representatives of governments of the world has recently, in December 2000, failed . Let us hope that the next conference in Johannesburg 2002 will recognise the importance of the environment and give it their support.

Good governance appropriate development and a process of disarmament must also be included in any CODE of CONDUCT. A vigorous campaign to stop the spread of Aids in the regions could also be included in the Development Programme. The Hague Appeal for Peace Conference (not to be confused with the Prime Ministers' conference mentioned above) attended by thousands of people, representing many dozens of **civil non-governmental** organisations from around the world (in July 1999), also made valuable proposals. These proposals are included in the Appendix, and are concerned with the Exploitation of the Third World, and Genetic resources affecting plants, animals and humans alike. All these guidelines should be in accord with the regions' own aspirations as expressed in prime ministers and civil conferences. They should also be conceived and encouraged with generous **grants**, not loans that may do more harm than good. These grants could be given under the new proposed UN Security Council and distributed by the UN Development Programme, which already has considerable expertise in development work. Insistence on "wage discipline and flexible labour markets and free trade" as is usual in the IMF and the World Bank today, have often created the conditions that have led directly to unemployment and social unrest, especially when the loans have to be repaid with interest. This is not to deny the need for wage discipline, or more flexible markets, but these can best be met through good governance, not the blunt tool of interest rates or the philosophy of "free trade" that is primarily designed to protect the rich countries.

3.4 THE UN ECONOMIC COUNCIL.

Perhaps the most important proposal to enable Regional Peace and Development Programmes to be implemented successfully comes from the **Commission on Global Governance**. This Commission was co-chaired by Sonny Ramphal, the former Secretary-General of the Commonwealth, Ingvar Carlsson, the former Prime Minister of Sweden and twenty six other eminent men and women from around the world. In 1995 they called for the creation of a **UN Economic Security Council** with "**at least equal status** (my emphasis) as the existing Security Council". They also called for the World Bank and IMF to be accountable to this newly formed Economic Security Council. If these recommendations were to be put into effect **and sufficient resources given** many of the world's problems could be tackled and resolved. Then only would the UN have at its disposal the financial means to restrict unrestrained free trade in regional areas and deal with the problems associated with globalisation. These **principles** must be dealt with at the **global** level but **implemented** locally and regionally.

All this is not to deny the need for something like the World Trade Organisation, about which there have been, quite rightly, large demonstrations, but to call for a more democratic and fair arrangements for the Third World. The WTO is a parody of what might have been achieved by a UN Economic Council. It has also progressively removed the power of individual countries to promote more self-sufficiency for the people at local level, not only in the Third World, but also in the Developed World...

3.5 FINDING THE MONEY.

There is no shortage of money, **given the political will**, which may be found only when there is a recognition that peace and security can only be obtained through co-operation, not armed force or the threat of force. For instance, the New Missile Defence proposal is estimated to cost at least $60 billion dollars, without taking into consideration the destabilising effect such a policy would have in generating a new arms race around the world. This proposal is now being seriously considered, even though the military is doubtful about whether it will be able to stop and destroy an incoming missile travelling at thousands of miles an hour in opposite directions, especially if decoys are used. Even if successful in its trials it is doubtful whether US security will be increased. The opposite looks more likely because, if implemented, the world will be starved of funds for real peacemaking, and real security, based on co-operation. Our hopes for the future will then be undermined and possibly destroyed.

These hopes are already weak enough as the US military budget, planned for 2001, is put at $310 billion (according to the US Foreign Affairs Journal of July/August p3), yet the US is finding it difficult to meet its comparatively small annual contribution to the UN. The US Journal concludes, "foreign policy will simply be impossible without more money."

If the US can find an additional $60 billion for its Son of Star War extravaganza, in addition to its already overburdened defence budget, surely it would be far better to use some of this money to directly remove the causes of war and create a sound basis of international law, as discussed more fully in chapter four on

MORALITY, JUSTICE AND THE PHILOSOPHY OF NATURAL LAW. The same reasoning also applies to the rest of the world.

3.6 A MARSHALL PLAN AND THE RULE OF LAW.

An excellent model for regional co-operation is the Marshall Plan that gave Western Europe peace, prosperity, and the rule of law, which few had dreamed of before 1939. After the Second World War it seemed as if the world leaders had learnt the lesson, that the Versailles Treaty was a vindictive one which many believe gave rise large scale unemployment in Germany and to the government of Hitler. Instead the most generous aid programme in history was initiated by the US, based on a spirit of generosity and enlightened self-interest, not experienced before or since. The motives were mixed, caused probably by the fear of Communism, but nevertheless the results were good and long lasting.

The importance of the Marshall Plan is that it gave all the countries of Western Europe **the incentive to co-operate and overcome their hates and fears** generated by the war. The result has been that we now have peace and prosperity and enforceable European Law in Western Europe, as formulated in the European Convention of Human Rights, the European Social Charter, the Council of Europe, and its newly formed offshoot the North-South Centre. Also the OSCE (the Organisation for Security and Co-operation for Europe). All these organisations, Conventions and Charters can be seen as the logical outcome of co-operation following the Marshall Plan. All these organisations are voluntary agreements committing each state to co-operate for enlightened self-interest reasons making it almost impossible for war to occur again within the EC.

3.7 AID

The cost of the proposed Star War Missile Defence system, however, is only a fraction of the trillions of dollars now being spent by countries world wide on defence under the illusion that it will give them security. If only 1% of this money could be diverted to the UN and the Economic Security Council, as proposed by the Commission on Global Governance, many regional programmes could be initiated in several of the flash points of the world threatening world peace. America holds the key because, according to the US Journal Foreign Affairs, (July /August 2000)

> 'on a per capita basis, each American contributes about $20 per year to development and humanitarian aid, compared to a median of $70 in other Organisation for Economic Co-operation and Development (OECD) countries.'

This discrepancy should not let other rich countries off the hook, especially the EC countries that have benefited so much from US generosity in the past. We should be following the Scandinavian countries example that have reached the UN target of 0.7% of its GNP for development while Britain has only reached about half this target. New Labour, promises to reach the UN target "sometime in the future". This promise must be kept and improved on.

The aim must be to establish, with adequate funds, the proposed UN Economic Security Council and then make its work widely known, especially to those regions in dire need. These regions could then apply for aid from the UN similar to the Marshall Plan, in the same way as countries now apply for assistance from the World Bank and the IMF. Then, providing a region accepts the disciplines of peace, as outlined in a CODE OF CONDUCT, aid would be forthcoming **not as a loan but as a grant**, as happened under the Marshall Plan. The incentive for the states within the region to co-operate with each other must, however, be generous enough for them to co-operate and bury their fears and ethnic hatreds. Also there must be the right conditions to ensure success so that money is not wasted on inappropriate schemes, hence the importance of good governance within a well-conceived Code of Conduct programme.

These conditions, unlike the present terms of the World Bank and the IMF that often undermine the social conditions of the country being helped under capitalistic principles, would be agreed under the auspices of the proposed new Economic Security Council. This Council would be democratically elected and include the Third World Countries. The general guidelines could form the basis of the **Code of Conduct** and be agreed between the UN Economic Security Council and the region concerned. The specific details of the Regional Plan must, however, be formulated by the region itself (as outlined by George Marshall in his speech initiating the Marshall Plan), otherwise they will be felt to be imposed by outside powers and therefore lose their value. The spirit of generosity must not be interpreted as a sign of weakness but of strength of purpose. Nor must it be interpreted as a bribe but as a sign of goodwill.

Once the regional development programmes begin to succeed more money could then be generated from each of the regions' own resources. More money could also be found from the much criticised multinational companies who are always ready and anxious to work in profitable and socially stable countries. All multinational companies must, however, work with a Regional Plan to avoid exploitation of the region, overlapping of work, and undue bureaucracy.

3.8 CANCELLING THIRD WORLD DEBTS.

Another valuable source of money could be found by cancelling Third World debts within the regional agreement and applying debt repayment to their social and economic development. As most Third World countries cannot repay their loans, their debts should be written-off as part of the overall regional agreement. This arrangement would be much more satisfactory than outright cancellation without any assurance of future peace and co-operation. For instance, some poor countries spend £1.70 per person per year on health care, but have to spend an insupportable £20 per person per year on debt repayments. Clearly if this debt burden could be lifted they would then be able to concentrate their energies on improving the social and economic conditions of their country.

3.9 ENLIGHTENED SELF-INTEREST.

All aid programmes must, however, have an important element of enlightened self-interest or they will never receive the support they deserve from the rich countries. Altruism is not enough. We must beware that the way to hell is sometimes paved with good intentions, and the way to peace is sometimes (as with the Marshall Plan) paved with mixed motives.

For instance, unless we remove the main causes of poverty and conflict, compelling refugees to seek a new life in the rich world, the situation now threatening the West's own stability, (as in Austria today), the problem will almost certainly grow worse. Removing the causes of poverty, war and refugees will cost us large sums of money, but much less than by leaving the problem to fester, deteriorate and possibly explode. Self-interest therefore demands that the West takes active steps to remove the causes of conflict and poverty that compels people to seek refuge in the rich world. Short-term immigration control is no answer to a long-term problem.

The Secretary-General of the UN has also proposed several other ways of financing the UN, which would be to the West's self-interest. For instance, he has proposed a universal levy on all arms sales to discourage the sale of armaments; also an international air travel tax in order to reduce pollution, which threatens the ozone layer and the world's climate. These taxes would provide the UN with additional money it so desperately needs, but they would also encourage more self-sufficiency and democracy at local level,(as discussed in the chapter about Globalisation) not only in the Third World but also in the Western World by reversing the dangers posed by globalisation. More self-sufficiency would also reduce the need to transport goods from one side of the world to the other, thus lessening traffic on our overcrowded roads, consequently adding to the world's pollution problem.

The well publicised "Tobin tax", advocating a tax on money transferred around the world at the touch of a button by speculators such as George Soros, has been supported by many influential people, including Soros, and many others in governments. A Tobin Tax must therefore be seriously considered, not only for raising money for the UN, but also for minimising the harmful effects to the world community caused by unregulated free-trade speculators. The destabilising effect on the world's currency of unregulated money on the stock exchange, and the unpredictable electronic financial markets (who know no allegiance to anyone but individual selfish gain) even threatens a financial world wide slump, as happened in the 1930's and nearly occurred again in the 1990's in Japan and other Asian countries. Economic stability must go hand in hand with providing the means for creating world-wide economic security. Poverty is not only an evil in itself but one of the underlying causes of war. Seen in this light Third World poverty is like an unexploded bomb waiting to be detonated.

3.10 REGIONAL AND INTERNATIONAL LAW

Regional programmes, by themselves, however, are not enough; they must include good governance and the creation of Regional and International law, based on the idea of making individuals responsible for their own actions. Regional Criminal Courts are already becoming a reality in Bosnia and in other parts of the world. These ad-hoc Regional Tribunals are to be commended as a stop-gap measure until a permanent International Criminal Tribunal is agreed… The importance of such a Court is that individuals who commit crimes, (as defined by the Nuremberg Principles), must be taken to the Court. This principle (of individual responsibility) is already well established **within** the UK and most civilised states based on human rights. There is no reason why it could not apply **internationally** as an essential arm of the United Nations. Most member states of the UN have already accepted the Nuremberg Principles, and the idea of a Permanent International Tribunal, but unfortunately the US, almost alone, is vetoing the idea. But it's an idea that must come if we are to have international law and peace.

This process is still in its infancy and must be nurtured within a favourable social, economic and political environment, at regional and international levels. The idea of a Truth and Reconciliation Commission, as pioneered in South Africa, must also be considered as a method of addressing crimes. Any individual found guilty in an INTERNATIONAL CRIMINAL COURT would then have the opportunity to go before a Truth and Reconciliation Commission or to the International Criminal

Court with the probability of prison and/or the confiscation of assets abroad and being made persona non-gratis anywhere in the world. Europe has even gone one step further, as a direct result of co-operation within the EC, and has created a European Commission and a Court of Human Rights, providing an opportunity for individuals to bring claims against their own countries. This right of individual petition to the European Commission could and should be emulated in other regions of the world.

Regional co-operation would also have the added advantage of making it possible for military and oil sanctions to be applied by the UN against any state within the region committing crimes against humanity, as in Bosnia and Africa, in violation of the Regional Code of Conduct. Regional aid should therefore be given for a limited period, say five to ten years on the understanding that if the spirit of the Code of Conduct is not adhered to, aid could be withheld and military sanctions imposed. Aid cannot be given unconditionally, but it must be seen to be fairly and justly administered in co-operation with the region concerned.

3.11 IMPORTANCE OF SELF-GOVERNMENT AND THE DANGERS OF GLOBALISATION.

It is essential, therefore, for all Regional Development Programmes to have the full co-operation of the states involved in the region in accordance with the CODE OF CONDUCT, already agreed by the states **before** their application for development aid is made. George Marshall, in his speech in 1947 outlining the Marshall Plan, stressed the importance of involvement by the Regions' States and the need for them to feel it is an idea they can fully support by saying:

> "it would be neither fitting or efficacious for this Government (the US) to undertake to draw up unilaterally a programme designed to place Europe on its feet economically. That is the business of the Europeans. The role of this country should consist of friendly aid in drafting a European programme and later support of such a programme so far as is practical for us to do so. The programme should be a joint one agreed to by a number, if not all, European nations."

The dangers of globalisation have been discussed in another chapter but perhaps it is sufficient here to say that the principle governing the future should be one based on co-operation not unbridled competition.

REFORMING THE SECURITY COUNCIL AND THE GENERAL ASSEMBLY.

To enable all that has been said above to be implemented there must be a reformed United Nations based on the **six or seven Continents** of the world being represented in the **Security Council**. The **General Assembly** could then be represented by all the smaller regions of the world in place of individual country representation.

If this arrangement were to be made it would avoid all the squabbling that now takes place as to which nation-state should occupy a seat at the top table. It would also encourage co-operation between all states, and, being smaller and more representative, more democratic and fairer.

The present system, created by the victor states following the Second World War, is generally recognised to be outmoded and in urgent need of reform. The alternative proposed structure would be, similar to the organisation of the Olympic Games represented by the flag of regions.

I do not visualise all this happening quickly, but it could evolve as a natural outcome of Regionalisation as proposed in this book.

The reform, as advocated above, would overcome the problem of how to give fair and proper representation to all countries, big and small, wealthy and poor, and would encourage co-operation between them. Reform of the Security Council has long been recognised as essential, but all the proposals so far made by governments have failed to meet the criteria of fairness and democracy and have fallen foul of the veto. Continental and regional representation meet these criteria. It would also give more influence to the General Assembly as proposed by the Commission on Global Governance. These major reforms are long overdue because the present unfair system cannot last much longer.

3.12 REDUCING THE BUREAUCRACY IN THE UN

The decentralisation of the work of the UN would also overcome most of the present bureaucracy associated with UN's work, which is at present directed from its centralised offices in New York and Geneva. Instead its work should be regionally based helped by a well-qualified Secretariat similar to that provided for under the Marshall Plan chaired by Lord Franks. The same problem of centralisation also affects most of the NGO agencies when they should be working in conformity with the regional plan. For aid to be effective these agencies must be based in the region being helped in co-operation with the agreed regional programme. An expert Secretariat must therefore be appointed to or by the region to avoid overlapping and inefficiency, and ensuring co-operation.

Well-conceived regional Plans could avoid many of these problems and be implemented in a matter of months, as happened under Lord Franks' Chairmanship when the Marshall Plan was instituted on the directive of the European Foreign Secretaries and Prime Ministers of Europe in 1946, work that subsequently became the Organisation for Economic Co-operation and Development (OECD) we know today. (see Appendix for an extract of Lord Frank's speech in 1978)

This vision proved to be a practical and visionary plan for Europe, so why not something similar for other regions of the world today? Bilateral aid to individual states has been inadequate, and so too have most of the many economic programmes based on globalisation and unfettered ill-conceived free trade. Even the many splendid proposals made by the UN Secretary Generals and other organisations, mentioned above, have failed, mainly for lack of support. Instead we need to offer an adequate **structure** for regional co-operation and a world governed by universal principles that are implemented regionally and sub-regionally, based on co-operation and the rule of law. The world is desperately in need of a new vision that gives hope for the future and the regional idea could be the answer.

4 Morality, Justice and the Philosophy of Natural Law.

4.1 INTRODUCTION.

Understanding the philosophy of Natural Law is a subject of the utmost importance because it gives meaning and purpose to our struggle for peace upon which everything depends. Despite its long history, however, going back to before the days of St Augustine and even the Stoics 300 years BC, the notion is full of ambiguity and has declined until recently. Fortunately it is now receiving a resurgence of interest because of the renewed perceived connection between law, morality and religious ethics.

The reason for its decline may be because of its past close association with the idea of God and the decline of religion since the Enlightenment and Age of Reason, and the popular belief that science has all the answers to all our problems. The truth is that we have thrown the baby out with the bath water. Instead, we need to harness all these understandings about God, reason, and science, in order to create a trinity of belief leading to a wholeness of purpose and meaning and to give us a sense of direction, based on experience, as outlined later in this chapter.

Although we can all see Nature around us and appreciate that there must be some underlying laws upon which Nature depends, it is not so easily understood how this affects our behaviour and the laws we make to govern ourselves. Nor can the idea of Natural Law be easily defined as it is based on feelings about justice arising from our inborn sense of right reason, moral values and experiences gained from our social, economic and physical environment. It seems, therefore, that Natural Law *is more a philosophy based on non-violence, truth, reason and Natural Justice and common sense from which statute law grows as a natural consequence.* At the risk of over-simplification therefore may I offer a few of my own personal thoughts on the subject, based on some of the well-known sayings from past and present philosophers. I have also taken the liberty of using capital letters for Natural Law because personally I find God in all Nature.

4.2 UNDERSTANDING NATURAL LAWS.

I suggest law may be considered within several broad categories.

First, we have the laws of science, such as Newton's law of gravity, which keeps us firmly attached to the ground and dictates that the apple falls to the earth from the tree.

Secondly, we have the man-made laws of government we obey daily and which are easily recognised in everyday life in our dealings with the police, and in the many hundreds of laws about taxation and criminality for instance. Understanding the basis of these man-made laws of government and how they depend on the climate of opinion, leads us to discuss the third category. In this sense all law depends on understanding the philosophy of Natural Law.

The third concept is where there is no answer in international law to a particular problem. There is a gap known by international-al lawyers as the question of 'lacunae' which can be filled only by what is called "normative decisions", defined by Oxford Dictionary as "establishing a norm or standard". This view rejects the classic idea of law as being 'neutral'. The decisions, to be taken (according to Rosalyn Higgins, a judge in the International Court of Justice, in a talk given to the Forum for UN Renewal on June 18 1999) are:

> "unashamedly for the realisation of values. The values of the international law system include such matters as peace, stability, and the realisation of human dignity... One cannot expect a specific 'rule' to deal with every single un-thought-of question any more than one can in domestic law. All one needs are relevant norms – that are guides to lawful behaviour – that one can then apply to the circumstances to which a court has not YET been called upon to apply them".

Morality, Justice and the Philosophy of Natural Law

The question then arises as to what are these "relevant norms that guide us to lawful behaviour"? I suggest they arise as a natural consequence of co-operation involving our own individual self-interests and our natural instinct to help the community. They are based on a combination of values, morality, a sense of justice and right reason supported by scientific understanding and should grow naturally and organically in harmony with nature as reflecting the mind of God. Although we may not know the mind of God directly, we can study His laws as perceived in Nature, including all the natural world and our ecological relationships to the whole of Nature. The world is one ecological integrated living organism and what affects a part affects the whole. We are what we are partially because of our genetic inheritance, partly because of our environment and past experiences, and partly because of our own free will, determination or education. Our future therefore depends on understanding the past and relating it to present day conditions. We cannot do much about our genetic inheritance but we can change our environment and our relationships with Nature, which can transform our behaviour for the better . The latest genetic "breakthrough" promises much but takes us into unknown territory with possible unforeseen and disastrous consequences. As with nuclear physics this is an area best treated with caution, at least until far more is known about its long-term consequences over many generations.

The survival of the fittest is also a basic Natural Law. All life is subject to this law from the microbe and insect world to the jungle world of the wild animal; the one important difference to humans is that few other animals kill their own species; usually **they co-operate in order to survive** and only kill other species for food or to protect territory. Only in very exceptional circumstances do animals kill and wage 'war', as we know it, on other animals of the same species. They have learnt how to ritualise conflict in much the same way as some primitive peoples have learnt to ritualise their conflicts. This lesson is described more fully by Ruth Finnegan in her chapter, Peace and Conflict in Non-Industrial Communities. (See Foundations of Peace and Freedom, Ed Ted Dunn).

Jesus illustrated this law of survival in his parable about the seed sower. Some seed, he said, fell on stony ground and withered away, but some fell on good fertile soil and flourished. Similarly our behaviour is dictated by whether our environment, and the conditions in which we are nurtured from birth, are conducive to good behaviour and relationships or not. This is reflected by the government we elect and consequently the laws we enact, a process, which may be called Natural Law. Obedience to these laws of Nature involves dealing with the **underlying causes** of crime and war and provides the concept of law in times of peace.

Unlike the animal world, which reacts instinctively to its environment, we humans have the power of reason, and can either work in harmony with the laws of Nature or ignore them in our selfish short-term, get rich policies. The road to hell is sometimes paved with the best of intentions, but we have a clear choice: either our behaviour is dictated by irrational feelings as a result of our sick society, or determined by reason, wisdom and justice, which taken together, are capable of creating a healthy and favourable environment, from which grow naturally the peace and the laws we make. Creating the right environment, or culture of peace, is the over-riding need for today's world. If this is true then it is essential that we seek to create the fertile soil and the environment upon which our feelings depend. Our task therefore is to understand these laws of Nature and implement them through government.

A fertile soil, however, is not enough because the structure of government is also of vital importance at local, national, regional and international levels. Ask any farmer and he will tell you that there is a time for cultivating and a time for rest and patience until the weather is right "to get on the soil". This is what may be called "working with Nature". The same is true of politics. An idea may be before its time, or (as Shakespeare said), "there is a time in the tides of the affairs of man which taken at the flood leads on to fortune". Our task today is to prepare the soil for tomorrow's growth.

The rule of law therefore, is the result of our social, economic and political environment, which, taken together with our experiences of

Morality, Justice and the Philosophy of Natural Law

life, based on morality and sense of justice and fairness, forms the basis of our national legal system. Natural Law is often called upon in courts of law in cases that cannot easily be defined by statute, or case law, but which nevertheless demand reason and common sense and is called Natural Justice to cover the "gap" in the substance of international law, as discussed in the 'Lacunae' argument mentioned earlier.

Justice, however, must be tempered with mercy, as is well illustrated in the Merchant of Venice where Shylock demands his pound of flesh "nearest to the heart". Natural Law and Natural Justice may therefore supersede statute or common law, which is constantly changing as new revelations about faith and ethics affect public opinion. Slavery, for instance, was, until comparatively recently, supported by law but is now illegal. Understanding the basis of Natural Law therefore provides a sound foundation for all legal or national law. Nuclear war is also now on the point of becoming illegal as the judgement of the World Court at The Hague in 1999 indicates.

There are two further examples of Natural Laws in action, which we obey daily, not only because of reasons of enlightened self-interest reasons, but also because they are in accordance with right reason, justice and common sense, as believed by many international philosophers and others, as discussed later.

First, the example of the Highway Code. The Highway Code could not be enforced effectively unless it commanded the overwhelming support of the majority of the population. We recognise that to get from A to B we must obey the rule of the road and keep to the left etc. The police have a duty to enforce these laws for the benefit of everyone and they are accepted as fair because they are obviously for our own good. In other words the law must be based on values that are universally respected or it will not be obeyed for long. Law based only on force may subdue but it creates a feeling of resentment and is then seen as a tyranny. Instead of being a force for good it is then a cause of further conflict. Many idealistic wars from the Crusades to the recent 'humanitarian' wars in Iraq and Kosova, have left the seeds of further conflict. Most conflict today is caused by a sense of injustice usually based on ignorance, or because there is no recognised way of resolving disputes peacefully – hence the need for this book.

A second example of obedience to Natural Laws is that of an orchestra where all the members have the same aim – to produce good music. To achieve this objective the players must accept the disciplines involved, especially the authority of the conductor, who in turn must conduct in accordance with the score. Also, all members of the orchestra, including the conductor, must learn the skills of playing an instrument. These are the bare essentials for good music, willingly accepted by all members of the orchestra. I suggest similar disciplines apply to our national and international life, especially in the UN, and why the idea of God, the author of Nature and the score, is so important as a guide to the future.

4.3 JURIES AND THE RULE OF LAW.

The concept of Natural Law is also a response to our instinct for justice and fairness. As children we often hear the cry, "it isn't fair", and this cry persists throughout our lives whenever we encounter injustice. Without this instinct civilisation would soon come to an end. All good law depends on this understanding. This cry for justice and fairness is reflected by the decisions by juries in recent years over-ruling the advice given to them by the judge. This trend was begun in 1670 when William Mead and William Penn persuaded the jury that they were not guilty despite the judge locking the jury up for two nights without "meat, drink, fire or tobacco". Even then the juries still stubbornly stuck to their verdict despite being fined. Ultimately the right of the jury to give their verdict according to their conscience was granted and Mead and Penn were acquitted. This verdict has since become the foundation stone upon which the trial by jury has rested. Lord Devlin, one of our great law lords, is said to regard the juries right to bring in a perverse acquittal as;

> "one of the glories of our jury system". It gives, he said, "protection against laws which ordinary man regards harsh and oppressive…an insurance that the criminal law will conform to the ordinary man's idea of what is fair and just. If it does not, the jury will not be party to its enforcement."

Several more important cases in recent years have supported this right of juries to place more importance on fairness and right reason than on the strict obedience to the letter of the law. For instance, Clive Ponting, a senior Ministry of Defence official, was acquitted for revealing to an MP that government ministers had misled Parliament over the sinking of the Argentine warship General Belgrano during the Falklands war. There was no doubt that Ponting had infringed the Official Secrets Act, nevertheless the jury acquitted him. Even more striking was the acquittal of Pat Pottle and Michael Randle on a charge of helping the Soviet spy George Blake to escape from Wormwood Scrubs prison in 1963, despite the judge's clear-and legally correct-instructions that the two men had no defence.

Similar decisions by the juries have been made when Pat Arrowsmith was charged under the 1934 Disaffection Act for leafleting troops at Aldershot, and Lord Melchett the executive director of Greenpeace, and 27 other environmentalists who trashed a field of genetically modified maize, were also acquitted by juries. Perhaps more importantly, for the cause of peace, Sylvia Boyes and Keith Wright, the anti-Trident activists were acquitted in November 1999 by the jury after pleading that their actions (to cause deliberate damage to a Trident nuclear submarine) were necessary to prevent a greater evil, and because nuclear weapons were immoral and in breach of international law (see Guardian 22 January 2001)

In all these cases the narrow legal interpretation of the law would have found the defendants guilty, but because the juries decided to use their reason and common sense, they ignored the direction of the judge. It is upon this foundation that our freedom and liberties depend. It is also a good illustration of why Natural Law is more important than statute law, and why governments and courts of law over-rule natural justice at their peril.

4.4 CO-OPERATION AND THE RULE OF LAW.

We also desire and need freedom and a share of the good things in life but recognise that these benefits cannot be ours unless we accept the disciplines of co-operation, because, as John Donne said, "no man is an island". Government and our ability to create the good things in life would be impossible without the willing co-operation of others; co-operation by its very nature, calls for the rule of law. All co-operatives must have a rulebook which we accept willingly providing the rules are seen to be fair and in accordance with right reason and common sense. The structure of government must also have a good organisation, or what is more generally called, "good governance". Failure of governments to have a good **structure** of organisation and governance may lead to its disintegration, as is happening in Africa today. That is why it is vitally important for the Regional Organisations of the United Nations to be conceived as fair and ethical to all its members, and why a Code of Conduct (as outlined in another chapter) is important for any region receiving help from the UN. This must be workable, honest and reliable. All these restrictions we accept as part of our bargain for government stemming from enlightened self-interest reasons, and our willingness to sacrifice small, but important, degrees of freedom and sovereignty for the good of all.

4.5 THE CLASSIC DEFINITION OF NATURAL LAW.

All the above conclusions are in conformity with the classic definition of Natural Law as given by Hugo Grotius, the famous Dutch lawyer, who many today believe was the founder, in the sixteenth century, of the modern science of international law when he declared:

> "Natural Law is a dictate of right reason, which points out an act, according as it is, or is not, in conformity with rational nature, has a quality of moral baseness "(a sixteenth century term which I take to mean having a moral base) "or moral necessity; and that, in consequence, such an act is either forbidden or enjoined by the author of nature, God." (The Concise Encyclopaedia of WESTERN PHILOSOPHY AND PHILOSOPHERS, Unwin Hyman, Second edition 1991).

Also, according to J.G. Starke QC in his book, AN INTRODUCTION TO INTERNATIONAL LAW 1967 Starke says:

> "Grotius has had an abiding influence on the history of international law. His treatise was continually relied upon as a work of reference

and authority in the decisions of Courts and in the text-books of later writers of standing."

In other words I believe Grotius is saying that we can recognise God in all nature, and that if we **nurture nature** in every aspect of our lives, (including international relations), with truth and diligence, a healthy world will result. Failure to recognise this truth can be seen with regard to the environment where long-term benefit is often sacrificed for short-term gain. It is equally true with regard to our economic, spiritual and moral values. We often talk about "nurture" and "nature" as either or, or as two separate parts of our being when we should be considering them as complementary. In other words Mother Earth needs nurturing and caring for as much as any child.

4.6 SCIENCE AND THE RULE OF LAW

The world famous scientist and biologist, Thomas Henry Huxley,(1825-95), whose monumental interests spanned both biology and philosophy, supported Grotius's weighty pronouncement about Natural Law (above) when he said, in the book, INNER LIGHT, (Gear Allen & Unwin 1946)

> "Science seems to me to teach in the highest and strongest manner the great truth which is embodied in the Christian conception of entire surrender to the will of God. Sit down before fact as a little child, be prepared to give up every preconceived notion, follow humbly wherever to whatever abysses nature leads, or you shall learn nothing. I have only begun to learn content and peace of mind since I have resolved at all risks to do this."

Alfred Russell Wallace, the great naturalist, challenged the orthodoxy of the time, and, with Darwin, established the idea of Natural Selection. Wallace also had a great respect for Huxley but he became unpopular with the establishment of the day because he believed the survival of the species depended upon **co-operation within** the species, whereas Darwin allowed his theory to be used by others to justify Thomas Hobbes belief that people are inherently selfish and brutish and that competition, capitalism and war is the natural outcome of Nature. This misuse of Darwin's theory of evolution may have been the reason why Western civilisation continued the fatal path of competition, conflict and war at a critical period of our history and why war is justified today. It is of course true that the survival of the species depends on one species living upon another, but each species also depends on co-operation within the species to survive. Very few species kill each other as an act of organised war but depend on **co-operation within** the family and a favourable environment for survival, factors that are well within our capacity to control once we have learned to obey the laws of Nature. This principle is endorsed by Dr. Ruth Finnegan, a Senior Lecturer in Comparative Social Institutions, (referred to earlier) who says, concerning primitive peoples, that their conflicts are "regulated and limited…through the use of mediators" Today's, so called more advanced civilisations must learn to do the same through economic co-operation and International Courts of Law.

The ideas of Wallace, based on the same observations as Darwin, have more recently been looked at again and confirmed by others such as John Ruskin and William Morris, and today by social scientists such as Dr James Lovelock who coined the concept of 'Gaia' and the 'evolution of life'. Teilhard de Chardin's philosophy also embraced a similar concept, which he called 'Omega', or "evolution in which matter and spirit come together within the whole universe". The ecology movement is also based on the inter-relatedness of all nature and that what affects the part affects the whole. This is not to deny the role of **enlightened** self-interest because without this element (for example in the United Nations), it is doubtful if any progress can be made. But short-term interests, based on quick profits, or emotional outbursts stimulated by the press, all too often obscure the long-term perspective.

The idea of Natural Law goes back much further to the Stoics, which according to Macmillan's Concise Encyclopaedia, was:

> "a philosophical school founded about 300 BC in Athens…Stoics believed that God (identified with reason) was the basis of the universe, that human souls were sparks of the divine fire, and that the wise man lived 'in harmony with nature', the basis of the universe."

This view about Natural Law was later supported by Cicero the great Roman philosopher, who studied Greek philosophy and later had such a profound influence on Roman culture, thought and law. It is claimed by some that Cicero and Aristotle were two of the greatest philosophers of all time. Today their ideas should again be taken seriously.

The idea of Natural Law has more recently been included in the idea of "Pantheism" (not to be confused with Paganism) by the Irish writer John Toland in 1705, based on the words "pan" (or all), and the word "theos" (or God). According to Paul Harrison the author of the book THE ELEMENTS OF PANTHEISM, (Element Books 1999),

> "If you love Nature, if you see divinity in all things, then you may well be a Pantheist. Pantheism is the belief that the universe and Nature are divine. It is a belief shared by great thinkers throughout the ages…and informs many of the world's religions and philosophies."

4.7 NATURAL LAW AND THE NATURAL WORLD.

Today the need to create a healthy world order based on the Natural World has never been greater. If only we could concentrate on basics, such as understanding Nature and ensuring, for example, that we have a pure unpolluted water supply, free from nitrogen and other farm chemicals, unpolluted air free from car emissions, and a good food supply based on organic methods, it is probable that many of the physical diseases we suffer from would be overcome. Elm Disease, Foot and Mouth disease and many more, should be a warning to us that all is not well with our environment. The same principle applies to national and international political affairs, and perhaps even more importantly, to our relationships one to another based on competition, when it should be co-operation.

Joseph Lister, a professor of surgery, who introduced the idea of asepsis and the prevention of infection by the utmost cleanliness, probably did more good than all the medicines later invented. But cleanliness is not enough if we still ignore the laws of Nature by polluting our water with nitrogen, poisoning the air with petrol fumes, and our food with insecticides, fungicides and fertilisers that upset the balance of Nature.

Ignorance about the Life Force that is within us all, is fundamental to all living plants and animals, is probably the root cause of so many of our problems. Because we cannot know where this life force comes from, or isolate it in the laboratory, (despite the genetic code) we assume it is not important and can be ignored in our search for progress, with the result that we are able to increase the yields of plants at the expense of their health and life giving properties. The reality is that unless we learn to nurture this life force within us as individuals and in our community, all our efforts to bring peace will fail.

Much progress has been made, however, in our understanding of hygiene and cleanliness and we have overcome many diseases, such as typhoid and dysentery as a result. Unfortunately, because we have also been so anxious to sterilise everything we have hindered the natural process of gaining immunity or resistance by having contact with harmful germs at an early stage. Gaining immunity depends, therefore depends on creating a healthy body in accordance with natural laws of health making it capable of being able to withstand the onslaught of disease when it occurs. We have all too often adopted short-term policies based on quick results that disregard the long-term laws of Nature, as understood by organic growers, with the result that our natural immunity to disease has been undermined over the long term. The ideal must be to create the conditions favourable for good health to enable the phagocytes in the human body to overcome the germs of disease from within without resort to drugs, insecticides, or artificial fertilisers.

This principle, based on long-term permanence and positive health, must also apply to international relationships. The lack of understanding about this law, or philosophy, is undoubtedly the cause of many conflicts. In other words the world community has within itself the ability to acquire an immunity to resist and overcome disease provided that the basic laws of Nature are understood and obeyed and we live in harmony with them. More importantly, if we live in accordance with these Natural Laws, based on reason and the concept of Natural Law, as outlined by

Grotious, this process provides us with a sound basis upon which to enact the laws of government.

This principle of faith was clearly outlined by St Paul when he called upon us to overcome evil with good; also by the new commandment of Jesus, "to love one another". Jesus's whole life was based on this philosophy; but he also added, "the first commandment is to love God" which I believe can best be seen by obeying the laws of Nature. Some people would perhaps call this a belief in Pantheism, (as mentioned earlier), or, as the Oxford English Dictionary defines it as, "that God is in everything and everything is in God". This idea corresponds with my Quaker belief, "that there is that of God in everyone", and that God is a Spirit that must be nurtured, even in our enemies.

4.8 THE POWER OF LOVE, OR THE LOVE OF POWER.

Today's political philosophy is usually the opposite to Jesus's teaching. Instead it should be based on the power of love, and Gandhi's concept of Satyagraha – the power of truth. These teachings have today been turned on their head to become the love of power. As a result, we all too often seek to treat the symptoms with short-term answers, when we should be understanding and treating the causes within a long-term perspective. Such a distortion can be seen in the case of war and preparation for war – a classic example of short-termism leading to long-term disaster. The same distortion can be seen in the total neglect (until recently) of organic farming, natural medicine, and peace research. The work of the UN also receives scant financial support compared to the expenditure on the preparation for war. The atomic bomb would never have been invented if we had a better understanding about the nature of peace. The same can be said about organic growing and natural medicine. Massive amounts are spent on drugs designed to kill germs or bacteria, but comparatively little on strengthening the natural immune system in our social, economic, physical and political environment to enable it to overcome the diseases of this world naturally.

Our educational system must therefore include the idea of **Education for Life**, as outlined in a later chapter, in all its manifestations in its curricula. If this change could be realised, the cost to our National Health Service could be drastically reduced. The causes of war could also be removed and the institutions of peace established with consequent savings on our Defence Budget. The same principle applies to peace research, a study that has only recently been accepted as important to world peace. Our objective therefore must be to define our philosophy based on working in harmony with Nature; only then can we provide the clear guide lines so urgently needed for our scientists and politicians. For instance, Einstein, the great scientist and physicist, and partly responsible for the nuclear bomb, later said, "if I had only known I would have been a locksmith".

4.9 ANOTHER DEFINITION OF NATURAL LAW

Another important definition of Natural Law was made by Henry Bracton, a great lawyer in the thirteenth century, when he declared that:

> "The king ought not to be under any man, but he ought to be under God and the law, since the law makes the king. Therefore let the king render to the law what the law has rendered to the king, namely dominion and power; for there can be no king where will prevails and not the law." (THE FOUNDATIONS OF FREEDOM by D.V.Cowen. Oxford University Press 1961)

In this book Cowen traces the origins of Natural Law from the Greeks and Roman thinking to its influence in modern history. Here we have it clearly stated that government under the law is very different from unfettered power based on violence. Only when the king or government is under the law is it possible for the king to govern for, as Bracton says, "there can be no king where will prevails and not the law". The Magna Carta, the basis of British freedom, was also based on this principle, i.e. that the law must be above the king. The idea of an International Criminal Court and the South African experience based on a Truth and Reconciliation Tribunal are also important steps in the right direction. The problem facing us therefore is how to reconcile freedom with power, and unity with diversity. In other words, how can we create something greater than either unity or diversity alone can attain. The Quakers put this idea well by saying, "in essentials unity, in non-essentials diversity, but in all things love". The problem of how to combine unity with diversity can clearly be seen in all nature where there is both harmony and beauty. The delicate balance of Nature must be seen in this context.

This problem is reflected in many other aspects of life today where we seek to be wanted as members of the community, yet at the same time we all need to feel an individual, each with a personality that wants to express itself, to find meaning and purpose in life. Our task must be to discover and develop the wisdom to find and then create the **structure** of organisation to enable these feelings to find a peaceful expression to enable us to live in peace in our social, political, and international relationships, as discussed further in the chapter, Reform the UN.

4.10 GOD, WONDER, LOVE AND LIFE FORCE.

Unfortunately the word God has so many different meanings, that I believe it would be helpful to substitute the words, "truth", "spirit", "ecology", "Nature" or "Creator". Many also believe that "where love is God is", and that, "there is God in everyone". I go one step further and believe that "there is that of God in all living things", even though it is impossible to know where that spirit or life-force comes from. What is indisputable is that there is a spirit, or life-force, which for want of a better word, some call God, and that it must be nurtured with loving tender care or disease will occur. Biologists and evolutionists may inform us how we evolve but they cannot tell us why, or where the spirit, soul, life-force or consciousness comes from; it is all beyond our understanding and perhaps always will be. Nevertheless we can seek to live in harmony with the laws of Nature we observe around us and this is why a holistic approach to peace and human relationships is so important. Nevertheless, I hold that there must be some power or influence in the universe that makes it all possible. I cannot believe that 'life', with all that word implies, happens by chance. Most people, including those who believe in evolution, must, at some time, have a sense of wonder at the beauty and order in all Nature.

Evolution does not answer all our questions. The most evolutionists can do is to describe the workings of Nature from the beginning of time. They cannot explain the mystery of life and death or that there must be some power, or mind, or life force, behind it all. Today Britain has become a country without a faith with no real sense of meaning, purpose, direction or philosophy. Competition in a materialistic world has become our religion to the neglect of community and spiritual values. Materialism based on competition is an empty shell impoverishing our spiritual lives.

Thomas Paine, the author of 'The Rights of Man,' a book that has had such a profound effect on establishing Human Rights and its subsequent impact on all our lives, based his belief in Deism, which the Oxford Pocket Dictionary defines as "a belief in the existence of God, not as a revealed certainty of God, but as a hypothesis required by reason". This hypothesis, based on reason, appeals to me because I can see and touch and understand Nature, whereas I cannot believe in a personal God who is all powerful yet cannot, will not, interfere with the workings of Natural Laws. If there is an earthquake God will not interfere with the working of His own laws to prevent it happening, or, if we go to war and millions are killed, God will not intervene. Nor will God intervene if we ignore Nature's laws and pollute the world causing millions to suffer or if we act foolishly and selfishly and ignore world poverty. Yet there is a spirit of God that lives in us all, which we call love that transcends most of these difficulties providing we adapt our studies and reason to resolving them. In other words, if we act and live in accordance with God's laws, based on reason, love, and, understanding the laws of Nature, war and poverty can be abolished and even earthquakes, floods and pestilence can be minimised. Many floods for instance are caused by deforestation, and most wars from lack of understanding. The spirit of God can also be awakened by a spirit of generosity between nation states, communities and individuals. For example, the parable of Jesus about the boy offering his loaf and two fishes which led to the whole multitude sharing their food was a miracle that could be repeated today by the rich world giving freely within a well conceived concept to the Third World. The Marshall Plan is probably a modern comparable example of generosity of spirit for today, even if inspired by mixed motives.

The spirit that lives in us all was also captured by Jean-Jaques Rousseau, the great French philosopher, educationalist and romantic in the 17th century when he wrote the Social Contract, and who believed in the importance of feelings, beauty, and moral sense, all essential ingredients for a peaceful world. Wordsworth also caught this feeling for a beautiful world.

4.11 THE MORAL CODE

Today it is the tyranny of governments that threatens to destroy us, because, if a government acts outside the moral code, as defined by Grotius and Bracton in the earlier quotations, it forfeits its right to claim to be acting in the name of democracy and freedom. For instance, the bombing of Serbia without UN approval, and the subsequent killing of many civilians for so called "humanitarian" reasons, were illegal and outside the moral code. Law without a basis of morality may even lead to legalised robbery and theft disguised under the name of democracy, capitalism or free trade. For example, no longer do we allow the slave trade but instead support "globalisation" and free trade to the detriment of the Third World. Conquest of land is now uneconomic and the idea of empire building no longer approved. Instead we seek to exploit other countries economies for our own short-term gain. The essence of Natural Law may be said to live in the constant assertion that there are moral principles, which depend upon the nature of the universe and can be discovered by reason and right ordering. Cowen supports this belief by quoting the Roman writer Cicero who wrote in his, De Republica III, that "true law is right reason in agreement with Nature" and that "we are slaves of the law that we may be free". The influence of Cicero's writings on Republican Rome, and Augustus in creating a Commonwealth was, he says, "enormous" and may partially account for the long period of relative peace under Pax Roma (despite Roman dependence on the use of force), alongside the Roman concept of dual citizenship (as exemplified by St Paul in the Bible).

4.12 STRUCTURES AND DUAL CITIZENSHIP.

The idea of dual citizenship is discussed more fully by John Ferguson, a Professor of Classics, in the book I edited called, FOUNDATIONS OF PEACE AND FREEDOM. Dual citizenship provides an example of what may be termed good structural government and should be included in all federal or confederal systems of government. Roman citizenship, Ferguson says, "sought to break down intermediate loyalties, which we might call nationalism." Nationalism for Life, (as discussed by Peter Manniche in another chapter in Foundations of Peace and Freedom), is to be encouraged, but nationalism for power is the cause of war. The concept of dual citizenship is also discussed in the book, 'The History of Rome' by M. Cary (Macmillan) where he discusses the Augustus government by saying:

> "By its liberal policy of bestowing Roman citizenship upon the provincials it effaced the traces of former conquest and converted the Roman empire into a commonwealth where the way to the highest offices stood open to all educated men regardless of race or nationality."

Infused with the philosophy of Cicero and enlightened ideas of the Augustus government, Pax Roma was bestowed on the Roman Empire. Over time, however, internal fighting and poor leadership led to its decay. But the idea of dual citizenship and Natural Law, as expressed by Cicero, remain lasting legacies for us to inherit and put into effect today in the Regional Assemblies of the world, such as the EC, and in the UN.

4.13 CODIFYING, OR LEGISLATING FOR NATURAL LAW.

Fortunately, today, the attempt has been made to establish the moral code of our behaviour in the UN Universal Declaration of Human Rights, and the European Declaration of Human Rights. These Declarations act as guiding lights to governments' behaviour and have already become enforceable in national and international law. In addition we have the idea of an International Criminal Court to which individuals may be taken who have committed crimes against humanity, peace, and human rights. It is near becoming international law today, needing only the US and seven other small countries to support and ratify the treaty. It has already been overwhelmingly supported by 97 countries that are committed to its ratification. Full ratification would be a huge step towards world peace under the law.

The International Court of Justice at the Hague, the world's highest authority on international law, also confirmed, on 6 July 1996, that international humanitarian law applies to nuclear weapons and that their threat or use seem scarcely compatible with its requirements.

This ruling was a milestone in the development of international law and should become one of the corner stones of peace in the coming years, especially if supported by social, economic and political co-operation, based on Regional Peace and Development Programmes, (as outlined in other chapters in this book). Nuclear war would then be outlawed and peace become within our grasp.

But law, based on fear or force, is not good law. Force may subdue but unless it has a moral basis it cannot gain the loyalty of hearts and minds. All the bombs in the world will not give us the security we seek, in fact quite the opposite, (especially nuclear bombs that assure us of Mutual Assured Destruction, appropriately named MAD). Without a moral basis, founded on right reason and justice, law based on force is counter-productive. Violence begets violence. Here we come to the need for new structures in the UN to enable everything to be integrated within a holistic concept creating something greater than the sum of its parts. This is the reason why I place emphasis on the idea of Regional Peace and Development, the reform of the UN, and adequate funding for the UN. Structural regional organisations and good governance are vital for any successful resolution of conflict. The UN can provide the forum for creating **global principles,** but these are best **implemented regionally and sub-regionally.** Reality dictates that all the many aspects of peace and security cannot be determined globally. In addition to the UN Declaration of Human Rights we also need a UN Declaration of Human Obligations similar to those provided in the Appendix in the Hague Agenda for Law and Justice.

4.14 THE GROWTH OF LAW IN THE MODERN WORLD.

After the First World War it was realised that something must be done and the League of Nations was formed. "Never again" was the cry and world government was called for based on the idea of "collective **military** security", a concept that has proved to be an illusion and a sure recipe for "collective **in**security" consequently violating the basic principle of "moral baseness", as outlined by Grotius who many believe founded the modern science of international law. Reliance on war to keep the peace, even for humanitarian reasons, as in Yugoslavia, also destroys trust and confidence between countries. Ethnic disputes within states can best be resolved by dealing with the economic and social causes, not by war, which only increases the problem. Nor can trust and confidence be nurtured if countries continue to arm themselves with weapons of mass destruction that could be used against each other. World government, based on the deterrent idea of "collective **military** security", must be inherently unstable and almost guarantees a feeling of insecurity amongst its members, especially if power is concentrated in few hands. Trust, confidence and co-operation cannot be assured if they rest on a basis of fear and possible war. There will always be suspicion and fear, especially when excessive power is placed in the hands of one super-power. Even democracies, such as the US and the UK, are not immune to the temptations of power. As is often said, "power corrupts and absolute power corrupts absolutely". World governance based on co-operation and the devolution of power to the local level under the law must be the answer. World law is essential but it must be based on non-violent principles and that is why this chapter about Natural Law is so important.

4.15 THE UNITED NATIONS

After the Second World War another attempt was made to create a new world order and the United Nations was formed. Although the idea of "collective military security" was retained in its Charter, far more emphasis was placed on co-operation and the idea of collective **economic** security and human rights was born. As a result we now have a proliferation of UN agencies and Non-Governmental Organisations (NGO's) all working for these ideals, in conformity with the concept of justice and morality. The Secretary-General of the UN is seen as a servant and leader, not as a powerful dictator; long may it remain so. World opinion has gone a long way in the right direction but it is learning its lessons the hard way by using the UN only in the last resort when it should be approached first, based on the principle that prevention is better than cure, and a stitch in time save nine.

4.16 WORLD GOVERNMENT AND WORLD GOVERNANCE.

The contrast between world government and world governance is that governance is seen to be based on a 'bottom up' approach founded on co-operation and good administration. By way of contrast, 'world government' is assumed by many to be based on a 'top down' approach, dictated by a small appointed elite in the Security Council and inevitably dominated by one or more of the Great Powers. Good management of the economy is also an important feature of governance. The difference between government and governance has still not yet been resolved or fully understood, especially in the European Community and the United Nations. Government is vitally important in providing the guide lines for co-operation, but its power must be tamed and under the control of world law, hence the importance of the UN Declaration of Human Rights and the idea of an International Criminal Court because there can be no peace except under the law. The question then remains; what do we mean by law and why the idea of Natural Law is so important.

4.17 THE MARSHALL PLAN – NATURAL LAW IN PRACTICE?

Another milestone in the progress of mankind was the Marshall Plan, an idea in accordance with right reason, justice and morality – the basis of Natural Law as discussed in another chapter. It was also a good example of the working of enlightened self-interest conceived, initiated and implemented within a matter of months after the Second World War. It seemed as if the Americans had learned the lesson of the Versailles Treaty that the vindictive attitude adopted towards a defeated Germany after the First World War resulted only in sowing the seeds of the Second World War. Many believe that fear of Communism may have been the incentive for the generous Marshall Plan but whatever the motive, the structure that was put in place, and the spirit in which it was implemented, must be commended. Over 2% of the US GNP was given over a 3-4 year period, not as a loan to be repaid as is usual today, but as an outright **grant**. The main condition made was that the states of Western Europe co-operated and formulated an agreed economic programme **of their own**, subject to the approval of the US, which was readily agreed. (see Marshall's speech in the appendix). In view of the success of the Marshall Plan why cannot similar well-conceived integrated holistic regional plans be initiated in other regions of the world under United Nations auspices? For a fraction of the money spent on armaments, many regions in conflict, or suffering from poverty or natural disasters, could have their future assured. The structures of peace keeping/making organisations must therefore be organised in times of peace to help those countries, or regions, suffering from war or natural disasters. Many Third World countries are caught in an economic trap due to bad governance, war, or because of Third World debts. A well conceived integrated Marshall Plan for these countries and regions that include a Code of Conduct, would enable them to overcome these problems.

Because of the Marshall Plan there has been a remarkable growth of European international law based on right reason, moral values and co-operation, all culminating in the European Convention on Human Rights. The Council of Europe and the Organisation for Economic Co-operation and Development (OECD) have also played an important role in Europe's recovery directly as a result of co-operation, none of which may have come about if the Marshall Plan had not been offered. There are also many other Non-Governmental Organisations around the world all working for development but needing to be co-ordinated within well-conceived regional programmes. There much overlapping and confusion between UN Agencies Governmental Organisations that could be avoided through regional planning. All future Marshall Plan regional programmes could grow naturally and organically if financed adequately by the EC or the UN. Europe has demonstrated that states are willing to sacrifice a remarkable degree of sovereignty provided there is the incentive and the organisation to work in conformity with concept of Natural Law and the Natural Laws of justice, reason and common sense.

4.18 NATURAL LAW IN DOMESTIC AFFAIRS

It may help to relate the idea of Natural Law to our domestic affairs. The Scarman Report for instance, (see the Home Office Report chaired by The Rt Hon. The Lord Scarman, OBE, on the Brixton Race Riots of 1981) reveals that if the authority of the police is to be respected and obeyed, it must enjoy the co-operation of the public because without co-operation its authority is undermined and therefore of little real value. The Exeter Community Consultative Group Report published by NACRO in 1979 confirms the Scarman Report by quoting Superintendent Colin More as saying, "operating without community consent, direction or control is wasted effort". Force may subdue temporarily but is usually counter-productive. Scarman's Report therefore recommended the creation of "community policing" and all that implies in reconciliation and conciliation methods. Minimum restraining force may still be necessary but never deliberate killing; the arming of the police was therefore a retrograde step especially when it tends to discourage non-violent means of patience and diplomacy.

4.19 A SPECIFIC PROPOSAL FOR PEACE IN REGIONS OF CONFLICT.

The first requirement is for a UN Peacekeeping/making force, as advocated by Brigadier Michael Harbottle, the one-time former Chief of Staff of the UN Peacekeeping Force in Cyprus, in his book, PROPER SOLDIERING, calling for the army to be trained in reconciliation, conciliation and reconstruction work. Only the army, he argues, has the money, the equipment, the men, and the expertise to undertake large-scale refugee work and rebuilding the infrastructure of a devastated country. Special non-combative units of the army should therefore be trained in non-violent methods and be ready to go to regions of potential conflict at short notice. They should **not** be expected to become **peace-enforcers** because then they would be perceived to be associated with one side of the conflict and consequently lose their moral authority upon which everything depends. Once involved in military warfare a UN armed force soon find themselves on a slippery slope and quickly become involved in the conflict far beyond the original peace-keeping intentions. Instead the green beret of the United Nations should stand for the moral authority of world opinion. The use of armed force can very easily undermine that moral authority.

Second, there is a need for a Permanent International Non-violent Civil Peace Force. This proposal is still in its infancy but it has been commanding increasing support in the UN and the European community and the International Conference of Non-Government Organisations at The Hague in 1999. A Non-violent Civil Peace Force could be funded by the UN and by charities, and should be trained and financed to go anywhere and do anything in accordance with non-violent principles. The work of the Quaker Ambulance Unit in both World Wars and of the War Resisters and other peace organisations today provides experience to build on.

By themselves the above two proposals are not enough, however, but must be supported and integrated with a political answer based on the proposal for Regional Peace and Development Programmes, (which forms the basis of this book).

They must also be supported with a UN radio and information service able to broadcast accurate news in time of peace and conflict about the benefits of peace and reconciliation.

These proposals must be seen as an integrated whole if they are to succeed.

4.20 WAR IS OUTMODED

It may also be argued that violence,(as used by the British army in the past in India at Amristar, in Ireland on Bloody Sunday, and the Boston massacres in the US), had a direct counter-influence on events resulting in an explosion of anger against the British and the subsequent loss of British rule, thus confirming Bracton's dictum (as discussed on another page) that the "king must be under God and the law since the law makes the king." More recently war has become more and more outmoded as a means of settling disputes as the wars in Vietnam, Afghanistan and many other places have proved. These conflicts have dramatically changed the idea of war and it is therefore imperative that we find an alternative. Fortunately many important writings by world statesmen have made an invaluable contribution to this debate, especially the booklet AN AGENDA FOR PEACE by Boutros Boutros Ghali when he was the UN Secretary General; also AN AGENDA FOR DEVELOPMENT by the same author. Regional Arrangements command a chapter of their own in this book.

More recently, in 1997, a massive well documented Final Report by the Carnegie Commission called PREVENTING DEADLY CONFLICT, was published. This splendid book has been compiled by sixteen world leaders and scholars and discusses the alternative to war in depth and concludes,

First, that deadly conflict is not inevitable.
Second the need to prevent deadly conflict is increasingly urgent.
Third, that preventing deadly conflict is possible.
Finally the Report "looks at the strengths and weaknesses and the way in which international organisations might contribute towards developing an effective system of **non-violent problem solving** (my emphasis)."

Particularly relevant to this book are their conclusions that

"the potential of regional mechanisms for conflict prevention deserves renewed attention in the next decade…and we must begin to create a culture of prevention" (p151)…and that economic growth could only be achieved through international or regional co-operation" (p145).

importance of this Report by the Carnegie Commission is not only that serious study has been given to the subject, but because the need for such a study has been recognised by so many important world leaders, such as Cyrus R Vance, its chairman and one time US Secretary of State and by other important people such as, Shridath Ranphal – the former Commonwealth Secretary-General, Jimmy Carter, the former President of the US, and Robert S McNamara, the former US Secretary of Defence. This book is a revolution in the making.

4.21 COMMUNICATIONS, NEWS, EDUCATION AND NATURAL LAW

Another factor that influences the idea of Natural Law has been the remarkable growth in communications, especially news, education and travel. No longer is it possible for politicians to assume that the public is ignorant about what is happening around the world because knowledge and information is now instantly available to almost everyone. A new climate of opinion based on truth and understanding is being formed compelling all governments to take notice of public opinion. Unfortunately, as with all things, manipulation of the media, especially on the Internet and by news barons can be used for bad as well as good. Again we need a new vision or philosophy about where our values lie. UNESCO and the Council of Europe are already playing an important role in promoting the vision for a Culture of Peace but far more needs to be done in schools and the media. The call from the UN General Assembly for a year of Culture for Peace, and a decade for the Culture of Peace and Non-violence, are important steps in this direction, if implemented enthusiastically.

The world is now a village and what affects a part affects the whole. Education by itself is not enough but must be directed by wisdom and moral values. We can have the most educated people in the world but what will it profit them if they are ignorant of the most important values in life? Or, as T.S. Eliot says, "where is the wisdom we have lost in the knowledge?" Prime Minister Tony Blair is right about the importance of education, but education for what? Education for the material things of life is not enough and should, and must, include Education for **Life**, as discussed in another chapter. It is at this level that true peacemaking and true culture begin.

4.22 TODAY THE WORLD IS AT THE CROSS ROADS.

We have the choice of taking the road of law enforced by violence, or that of Natural Law based on non-violence. These two philosophies (of war or peace) are incompatible because they each demand and compete for the same economic and political resources. No man can serve two masters, and the demands of peace cannot be reconciled with the demands of war or the preparations for war. It is sometimes said there is nothing wrong with the UN but the lack of political will to make it successful. Fortunately change is taking place, perhaps faster than we realise, but, as with any great ship of state it needs time, so the sooner we decide to change course the better. The UN Secretary General Kofi Annan and many others are already calling for the reform of the IMF, the World Bank, and the Security Council, as discussed in the chapter 'Reform and Renew the UN'.

4.23 RECENT THINKING ABOUT NATURAL LAW.

Many modern eminent international lawyers and philosophers have already recognised the importance of Natural Law and have included it approvingly in their textbooks. But few people in the peace movement, or in the legal profession, seem to have fully recognised its importance to the resolution of peace – hence the reason for this chapter.

For instance, Lloyd's INTRODUCTION TO JURISPRUDENCE, a book now established as a leading book on the subject (Stevens 1995 fifth edition) has this to say about Natural Law:

> "We have in this edition given much greater attention to both the history and the philosophy of Natural Law thinking. This chapter is nearly three times the length of previous editions".

Lloyd in a subsequent Penguin book called, THE IDEA OF LAW, expands on the idea of Natural Law by saying:

"It (the universal faith of Christianity) was really the combination of Christian theology working upon a substratum of Greek philosophy and Roman law which fused into the medieval scholastic doctrine of Natural Law which has played so important a part in the legal philosophy of the West ever since."

J.L. Brierly in his book THE LAW OF NATIONS also supports this belief by quoting the words of St. Thomas Aquinas as saying:

"The Law of Nature was that part of the law of God that was discoverable".

Another book devoted entirely to the idea of Natural Law is by A.P. Entreves, a Professor of Government in the University of Turin and formerly in the University of Oxford, who says:

"For over two thousand years the idea of Natural Law has played a prominent part in thought and history. It was conceived as the ultimate measure of right and wrong."

The idea of Natural Law is also encouraged by Paul Sieghart in his book THE LAWFUL RIGHTS OF MANKIND Oxford 1996 in which he supports regional instruments, international treaties, covenants and conventions.

In all these books there is the constant reference to right reason, morality and justice as the basis of law and the doctrine of the good. Whether my interpretation of Natural Law is in accordance with these books must be for others to decide, but what is certain is that we have much to learn from their understanding about the nature and basis of law.

Chambers Twentieth Century Dictionary perhaps sums up what is meant by Natural Law where it says:

"Natural Law is a law of Nature: the sense of right and wrong which arises from the constitution of the mind, as distinguished from the results of revelation or legislation."

Perhaps the final word about Natural Law should be left to Cicero in his treatise ON THE STATE (1113), when he says

"True law is reason, right and natural, commanding people to fulfil their obligations and prohibiting and deterring them from doing wrong. Its validity is universal; it is immutable and eternal. Its commands and prohibitations apply effectively to good men, and those uninfluenced by them are bad. Any attempt to supersede this law, to repeal any part of it, is sinful; to cancel it entirely is impossible. Neither the Senate or the Assembly can exempt us from its demands; we need no interpreter or expounder of it but ourselves. There will not be one law at Rome, one in Athens, or one now and one later, but all nations will be subject all the time to this one changeless and everlasting law." (Cicero, Penguin Classics 1960)

Today it may be worth quoting Richard Falk, Professor of International Law, Princetown who, speaking at Nuremberg in 1983 said:

"The time has come to found a movement of political action that will impose international standards on the nuclear powers and bring the people of the world some hope of peace and justice."

5 Aid, Conditionality, Self-Sufficiency, Permanency and Globalisation.

5.1 HARMONY OF OPPOSITES

One of the most difficult questions we have to answer today is how to resolve the problems arising from globalisation with self-sufficiency and localisation. It is similar to the age-old problem of resolving the opposite ideas of chaos and order, unity and diversity, or individualism and world order. In other words, how to harmonise apparent opposites to create something better than either alone can achieve, is one of the major problems facing mankind today, and is made worse by the rapid increase in communications, especially transport and the Internet.

Trade today is usually regarded as a natural essential part of our lives to enable us all to live the "good life". But though modern technology makes it possible to transport goods cheaply from one corner of the earth to the other, it has also brought us many problems, such as crowded roads, air pollution, its impact on the environment, and road accidents. More importantly it has undermined our local communities and sense of belonging by centralising everything in the name of progress.

"Free" trade sounds fine in principle but in practice it has meant putting more and more power into the hands of the multi-[national] corporations, squeezing the small man out of business [... w]e are reaching the stage where half-a-dozen corpora[tions contro]l half the worlds' economy.

The problem of free trade also has a profound influence on world peace because no state wants the United Nations, or any other body, to intervene in matters that are essentially within its own domestic jurisdiction. Similarly no state want to have their freedom of action to trade limited or controlled. Freedom and trade are seen as sacred principles. Unfortunately this is not true because freedom, like peace, must be under the law and controlled or it will do more harm than good.

This is not to say that free trade is bad, but that trade must work within constrained limits. We do not want to return to the days before the 2WW when Germany and Japan waged war to enable them to have access to raw materials. Since then the world has opened up its markets, and empires with their closed and protected markets, have almost ceased to exist. Germany and Japan now have equal access to the world's raw materials similar to any other nation-states. But we have gone too far and now the huge corporations rule the world to the detriment to the world's poor. The World Trade Organisation, which should be able to control world trade, is seen by many to be under the influence of big business, with little regard to the much wider considerations of world peace, the Third World, and the environment. There are even wider considerations arising from the freedom by which international financiers are able to move currencies, (and consequently jobs and the financial stability of even a rich country), at the touch of a button. The bottom line is profit and survival and if necessary, damn the consequences.

The UN Charter, however, expressly forbids (under Article 2.7) the UN from intervening by saying that it cannot intervene, "in matters which are essentially within the domestic jurisdiction of any state" but goes on to limit this demand by saying, "this principle shall not prejudice the application of enforcement measures under Chapter VII". (Action with Respect to Threats to Peace, Breaches of the Peace, and Acts of Aggression).

We are thus faced with the problem of what to do if any one state believes that its sovereignty and independence gives them the legal right to deny any interference in its domestic jurisdiction. This right of sovereignty and independence has been used effectively by poor and rich countries alike from preventing conditions being imposed, especially on a backward state, with the result that much aid has been squandered and misdirected on inappropriate imports, or purchasing huge quantities of arms, or building grandiose public palaces. Aid has also been used to allow the state to help it to wage war on its neighbours. Clearly we need some better way of providing aid that is in accordance with the UN Charter without resort to "enforcement measures".

At the risk of repeating myself the answer to this problem must be founded on the principles of co-operation and enlightened self-interest in the UN and by the states giving and receiving aid, based on the **Precautionary Principle,** of 'a stitch in time saves nine', and the idea of Regional or Sub-regional aid before conflict. The idea of an International Criminal Court, where individuals who have committed crimes can be taken, must also be supported. So too must the idea need for Truth and Reconciliation Commissions.

The present situation has been made more complicated by the way in which trade has been implemented in the past by the IMF and the World Bank, often forcing poor countries to export their primary products (tea, coffee, copper, etc.) in exchange for expensive capital goods (machinery, armaments, medicines, etc.), at the expense of their social and economic situation. The principle of conditionality has therefore already been infringed by the IMF and the World Bank because when countries are in debt and impoverished they are in no condition to refuse conditional aid. All states, however, rich and poor alike, cherish their sovereignty and do not want to be placed under the rule of law unless they can see some tangible benefits. The World Trade Organisation has also been under attack for being too much under the influence of big business.

5.2 FREE TRADE AND GLOBALISATION

The UN Charter, denying states the right to intervene militarily without the authorisation of the UN, (in matters that are within the domestic jurisdiction of any state), has also clearly been violated in Kosovo. Even though the bombing of Serbia was claimed to be on "humanitarian grounds", it was against the wishes of most members of the Security Council and therefore illegal.

On the other hand the Charter clearly states that the Charter "shall not prejudice the application of enforcement measures". The question therefore remains as to what we mean by "enforcement measures"? Where do we draw the line between "giving in" to the state claiming sovereignty, and military enforcement? I suggest there is a third way based on social and economic and political justice and the idea of Regional Peace and Development. This idea is holistic in concept, founded on the 'carrot and stick' principle and could include military sanctions and the rule of law based on non-violent principles, as outlined in chapters 3 and 4.

The whole problem has been made more complicated by the poverty trap in which the Third World has found itself, and the continuing conflict between its own ethnic peoples, conflicts that drain their resources and undermine their social and economic base. Poor countries also have a balance of payments problem, made worse by their huge debts compelling them to export more of their **primary** goods, such as agricultural produce, at less than cost in a flooded, often subsidized market in order to obtain foreign currency, a sure recipe for social unrest. Unlike manufactured goods that can quickly be stopped production, primary producers are far more vulnerable and at the mercy of world market forces.

This arrangement suits the rich countries because they pay less for their imports and have a captive market for their exports. In a global market this policy is unsustainable and must be changed in forthcoming World Trade and UNCTAD Conferences where it is to be hoped more support will be given to the UN International Fund for Agricultural Development, or the UN Development Fund. Better still would be a new UN organisation to finance Regional Peace and Development Programmes.

The classical solution to the problems of debt and development by the economists in the rich world has been to demand that the poor countries reduce their social expenditure on health and their basic standard of living, to enable them to live within their income and have a favourable balance of payments, with the consequence of creating even more social unrest, poverty and unemployment. It is all done, from an orthodox economic point of view, with the best of intentions and what some Americans like to call, the "classical liberal tradition" based on free trade, but what others call "unbridled capitalism". This is not to deny a role for capitalism if based on worker control or in sympathy with the poor peoples' aspirations, but to recognise that unbridled capitalism is like a wild horse that must be tamed if it is perform useful work. There is also an important role for land reform based on the Henry George "site rent", or "land value taxation" system. Land reform goes to the heart of many of the world's problems.

Fortunately the IMF and the World Bank are now, (2002), looking at ways of providing aid to reach the poor directly, due to public pressure. Whether this good intention will be realised remains to be seen in view of the fact that the loans from the IMF and the World Bank have to be repaid with interest. Another initiative slowly being adopted is to cancel the Third World debts of the poorest countries, but whether this change will be implemented within well-conceived integrated regional programmes again remains to be seen. This policy, if fully implemented, could encourage co-operation between potential enemies, the most important change if peace is to be created. The new Lomé Agreement (now called the ACP-EU Contonou Agreement) goes some way towards this ideal, as discussed in Chapter 1, page 1).

These moves are all in the right direction but they go nowhere near to resolving the problem because the poor countries cannot compete with the rich countries over price for their primary products, or with their manufactured goods unless they pay starvation wages. When this happens it has the consequence of under-cutting the rich countries' industries and causing unemployment in the West. The free trade system also encourages industry and agriculture in the rich countries to export their mass production methods to the poor countries with the inevitable result that less labour is needed. This policy is especially true of agriculture in the Third World where modern technology can mean one man on a combine doing the work of hundreds. The result is mass migration in the poor countries to the cities, causing large scale unemployment, squalor, and social insecurity for the majority. No wonder the causes of social unrest, conflict and war are so prevalent in Africa and other poor regions of the world. It reminds me of the Enclosure Act in Britain in the 15th and 16th centuries that reduced the independent yeomanry (the backbone of England at the time) to become labourers or serfs, or being forced off the land with nowhere to go. The distress that followed led to serious rebellions in 1536 and 1569. Similar social distress followed the Industrial Revolution. In both these instances the changes were, from a technical point of view, desirable, but from a human point of view disastrous. Denmark, with its more enlightened government possibly because of it 'education for life' policy, as discussed in chapter 6, met the same challenges by providing social legislation to help those who suffered from the change.

5.3 SELF-SUFFICIENCY

The long-term answer must be to encourage more self-sufficiency and more co-operations, as advocated by Gandhi with his village industries, not only in the Third World but also in the rich West, and by rebuilding strong, self-reliant economies at local level within a regional and global context. Information Technology may help this process if it enables more work to be undertaken from home. Unfortunately, modern means of communication and cheap transport are encouraging greater concentration of power into fewer and fewer hands at the expense of self-sufficiency and long term good of all. This makes no sense from social, economic and environmental points of view. Globalisation is fast becoming the problem, made worse by the speed with which international financiers can manipulate the market and upset the economies of even the richest countries, as happened to Britain on Black Wednesday, and to Japan and other Asian countries in recent years; it may even affect the US if confidence in the dollar collapses due to the huge US debts. To illustrate the idea of self-sufficiency in an African context see the photograph I took in Ethiopia.

The idea of Self-Sufficiency for Africa and the idea of wealth being generated upwards from the grass roots, is well illustrated by a photograph I took in Ethiopia, showing a young African women spinning cotton for her dress, outside an African house I had built in a week, alongside a tree being sawn down to be used for fuel to burn to provide food for the hospital. We also planted several hundred trees for the future.

5.4 A TOBIN TAX

As a result of globalisation no country is immune from the threat to its economy. To help resolve this problem the economist James Tobin has lent his name to the proposal for an international tax to discourage disruptive speculation on the stock exchanges of the world and to stabilise currencies and lower interest rates. This proposal is gaining increasing support from governments and NGOs around the world. More importantly the tax would raise many billions of dollars for the UN to finance GRANT aided world development. Other tax raising ideas were proposed by Mr Boutros Boutros-Ghali, (when he was Secretary General of the UN) in his important booklet AN AGENDA FOR PEACE, most notably for a levy on the arms trade. It is imperative that additional funds, such as these, must be found to enable the UN to perform the tasks of peace and development.

More self-sufficiency would also reduce transport costs and pollution, which is causing so many problems in the environment, directly changing the climate of the world. In addition, only when people feel that they have more control over their own lives at the local level will they feel they belong to a truly democratic state and world community. Many social studies in trade and industry encouraging worker participation confirm this belief. More self-sufficiency would also encourage confidence in the local economy and in the financial cities of the world. The "informal economy", (often called the hidden or illegal economy) which already accounts for up to 50% of the economy in many countries in the Third World, should also be harnessed more effectively as an integral part of a self-sufficiency campaign in both the poor and rich world.

The need for more self-sufficiency is most acute in Africa where it is impossible for its agriculture and industries to compete with the West because of the huge debt around its neck, made much worse by conflict and war It is therefore important for African States to strive for local sustainability and self-sufficiency by providing better water supplies, more trees, land reform, alternative technology, rural education and more effective but low cost medicine based on the Chinese bare-foot principle. Money spent on large-scale capital equipment, such as providing a modern unsustainable high-cost modern hospital for the rich few, is of little long-term value if the country cannot afford its upkeep. Growth should come from a sustainable local economy, jump-started by generous Regional Peace and Development Programmes, financed by the UN.

The aims of sustainability are well within the grasp of all African states **providing** they receive help from the UN to enable them to rejuvenate their economies and learn to co-operate to emerge from the pit of despair in which they now find themselves.

The cost to the West would be negligible compared to that of allowing the present state of affairs to continue, not only in financial terms from the rich world, but also in the human cost of malnutrition, social deprivation and war in the poor countries. The one per cent Tobin Tax could easily transform this situation and remove one of the most important causes of poverty and war. 'War on Want' estimates that a 0.25 per cent Tobin Tax could raise $250 billion per year for the UN. This money could be used to encourage co-operation within the regions and sub-regions, and consequently support the basis of international law, the underlying theme of this book. It could also help to remove the stranglehold by international financiers over the economies of the world.

Unfortunately there is little profit to be made by the multinational firms in the short-term by supporting self-sufficiency in the Third World, and therefore, no incentive for them to invest. The UN should fill this need, or gap, because it would be to everyone's benefit in the long-term. Even the multinational firms, which require socially stable countries in which to invest, would benefit, providing they conformed and contributed to and within well-conceived long-term regional plans. Short-term aid to individual countries, which have no commitment to co-operate with their neighbours, or begin a process of disarmament, (as provided for in the Code of Conduct discussed in another chapter), invariably leads to long term-disasters and is usually a waste of money. This aid is often diverted to war purposes and used to line the pockets of the war barons of the West, or the prime ministers of poor countries.

'NAL SECURITY BASED ON CO-OPERATION ..,UCATION.

All this means a radical and fundamental change in our attitude towards peace and education, but so long as the prevailing view about security in poor countries and rich countries alike is based on military defence, the causes of war will remain un-resolved. Fortunately there are signs of change. and in the future we must seek to remove the causes of war and promote the institutions of peace with the aim of creating a new world order based on trust and confidence It is a battle for the hearts and minds of humanity. Reliance on war, or the preparation for war, is a sure recipe for creating a circle of fear, hate, and conflict. The alternative must be to use our spiritual and economic resources to encourage co-operation, trust, confidence and security.

The forces against change are formidable, especially from the arms industry, with their vested interests which has an enormous and unjustified influence on governments. It is estimated, for instance, that it costs £1 million for each worker employed on the Eurofighter, a plane that will be out of date soon after it is made. Not only is this a waste of money but it illustrates the urgent need to put similar monies to constructive purposes that will increase world peace and security and employment. Perhaps an even more formidable obstacle is the psychological one based on fear which can so easily be exploited by the popular press, supported by vast sums of money from the vested industries. History has also supported the idea of war, and has conditioned our minds to believe that there is no alternative, despite the fact that the systems of law and order already exist within Britain, the EC and most democratic states today. They should be copied by the UN to ensure peace through law founded on justice, and cooperation

It is imperative that we relate this alternative, of law, to murder, conflict and to international relationships, especially between neighbouring states within a region where most wars in recent years have occurred. If we fail, science has now created a situation where war could easily mean the end of civilisation. Unfortunately, science and the information explosion are increasing at such speed that even poor countries will soon have it within their power to initiate nuclear, chemical or bacterial warfare and consequential world disaster. Today, individual terrorists also have it in their power to kill thousands and possibly millions. On the other hand information technology provides us with the means to gain the understanding so essential for peace making. Unless we change the culture of society to one of peace, based on trust and confidence, it is only a matter of time before resentment at the vast differences between the rich and the poor will generate fear and envy and consequently create the conditions of war.

The West is also stirring up more and more resentment in the Moslem world by bombing Iraq and portraying the Moslem world as the enemy, made more inflammable by supplying Saudi Arabia and Israel with huge quantities of the most modern weapons which one day may be turned against us. Instead we should be encouraging these countries to support a Middle-East Regional Development Programme as an essential part of the work of the UN. A Middle East Regional Water Programme is urgently wanted and could be the means of providing a common purpose in which all states could co-operate, especially between Arab and Jew. But it is doubtful if this will happen without generous UN aid to give them the incentive although Saudi Arabia alone could probably finance the idea if it were to use its huge oil income for the purpose instead of using it for a wasteful defence programme encouraged by the West for its own vested interests.

The world could easily afford the money if it reduced its military expenditure, because in 1996 it was spending 900 billion a year on armaments at the expense of world development abroad and social and political security at home. Since then world defence expenditure has increased and the Peace Dividend does not seem to have materialised, or if it has the United Nations and the Third World have seen very little of it. The result is that the rich are getting richer and the poor relatively poorer. The alternative must be a process of disarmament based on world economic co-operation (not outmoded military security), to enable rich and poor alike to enjoy the fruits of co-operation.

Enlightened self-interest demands that we create a stable and economic world order based on fair world trade and self-sufficiency.

Today we live in a global world where what affects a part affects the whole. No person or state lives in isolation and it is imperative that we create a new world economic order based on green issues, especially self-sufficiency and non-violence, or we die from war, pestilence, pollution or other man-made short-term get-rich solutions.

5.6 A CULTURE OF PEACE

The realisation that there must be an alternative to war is now generally accepted and the League of Nations and the United Nations have attempted to provide the answer. Many people believe that the UN has failed. Others, that it is its members that have failed the UN. The reality is that so long as the idea of Collective Security based on the military prevails in the public mind, (as provided for in the UN Charter Chapter VII), so too will it prove difficult to change the Culture of War to a Culture of Peace. A Culture of Peace and economic co-operation could give us collective economic security, international justice and law, and should be a top priority for a well funded UNESCO.

Changing people's minds from a culture of war to a culture of peace is the major task for today and this fact has been recognised by the General Assembly's resolution calling for a Culture of Peace for the year 2000 and a Culture of Peace and Non-violence for the following decade. If acted upon vigorously by the governments and Non-Government Organizations of the world, this resolution could mark the turning point towards world peace, especially if linked to the idea of Education for Life as pioneered by Bishop Grundvig of Denmark (1783-1872) and which is still continuing in the Danish Folk Schools, as discussed further in Chapter 6. Peace begins in the minds of men and women and it is at this level that we must concentrate. This is why there is a separate chapter devoted to EDUCATION FOR LIFE in this book. It is perhaps no coincidence that Denmark now gives the most money to the UN (more than .07% of its GNP) for development and that Denmark's king continued to wear the Star of David in defiance of Hitler that led to a non-co-operation movement during the war.

There are many other hopeful signs of change. For instance, the proposed cancellation of Third World Debts and the failure of the

World Trade Organisation at its conference in Seattle must be welcomed. This is not to deny the importance, and the need for, the World Trade Organisation, but to emphasise the need for a changed emphasis regarding development.

5.7 A SEA OR MIND-SET CHANGE IN OUR PERCEPTION OF PEACE NEEDED.

Enlightened self-interest also means that it is in our own interests to remove the causes of war and conflict and to study the potentialities of non-violence as a means of resolving conflict. Peace and non-violence are no longer the preserve of the few but recognised by a growing number as a necessity for today's world. Gandhi taught us about non-violence and peaceful resistance and there has been an upsurge in peace research during the past 30 years. The prestigious Carnegie Foundation for instance, has launched an important study on the "potentialities of non-violence" in a mammoth study called, PREVENTING DEADLY CONFLICT. In addition past and present UN Secretary-Generals have written important Reports outlining non-violent alternatives to war, and the annual UN Development Programme Reports and the Commission on Global Governance, have issued valuable studies and offered a better way to implement development programmes. This is not to deny the IMF and the World Bank a rightful place providing they return to their original intentions agreed at Bretton Woods soon after the war – an idea based on Maynard Keyne's classic thesis about relieving unemployment by increased public spending providing it was non-inflationary. The idea of an International Criminal Court to which individuals who have committed crimes may be taken, is also a milestone in human progress and if implemented alongside Regional Peace and Development Programmes could outlaw war. The decision of the World Court at the Hague outlawing war, is also another milestone passed. Many other important studies have also been made, such as the writings of Erskine Childers, a Senior Advisor to the UN Director General, and Brian Urquhart, who worked closely with the first five UN Secretaries-General for Special Political Affairs. The Dag Hammarskjold Foundation in Sweden and the Ford Foundation in New York and the influence of the New Economic Foundation all indicate a profound change in the minds of those who hold positions of power and influence. The new millennium offers hope for the future. The work of the US Institute for Peace also holds out hope for a new turning point.

All these initiatives, however, call for more political will on the part of governments, particularly by the wealthy countries who have it within their power to finance the changes so urgently needed. Many of these initiatives do not demand large sums of money, but they do require a determination to support the UN and the rule of law. For instance, because the UN and the rule of international law was by-passed in favour of NATO during the Kosovo crisis, world disarmament and the rule of law was put in serious danger.

Fortunately the forces for peace and sanity, as outlined above, are quietly but steadily gaining strength fortified by new technology such as the international independent TV/Internet service, an idea already up and running, led by Canada, under the name of WETV ("We the People and the Whole Earth"). It is now operating in thirty-one countries and is funded by Scandinavia, Netherlands, Switzerland and Austria. The time is overdue for the UN to have its own radio and TV World Service, especially in regions of conflict.

By way of contrast the unilateral action by NATO to bomb Serbia encouraged and gave the green light for Russia to wage a similar war in Chechnya to the detriment of peace and international law all over the world. In both instances, many billions of pounds were spent waging war ($30 billions for Kosovo alone), destroying towns and thousands of lives in the process and generating even more fear and distrust just where trust and confidence are most needed, the result being worse than the evils it sought to overcome. We now have made the task of reconstruction, reconciliation and conciliation made even more difficult.

Hopes rose when the Prime Minister Tony Blair talked about a Marshall Plan for the Balkan region and this was followed by Chris Patten's speech as EC Commissioner for the Balkans mentioning the same idea. Several years earlier on May 28 1997, President Clinton appealed to the West to complete the task begun 50 years earlier for post war construction and to help make Europe a united democratic and prosperous region. All these good aspirations have not, unfortunately, been fulfilled though a welcome start has been made. Russia should also be involved as its near neighbour.

The direct result of the Kosovo war has been to encourage and give legitimacy to the new prime minister Putin of Russia to wage war in Chechnya and threaten to increase his country's military expenditure by 50% if the current disarmament proposals fail. Taken together with the US Star War Proposal by the US, it is obvious that the future looks very bleak because there simply cannot be the financial resources or the political will to go in two opposite directions at one and the same time. If only a few of the millions spent on defence could be used to remove the causes of war, as outlined in this book, peace could be within our grasp.

5.8 CONDITIONALITY AND NON-INTERFERENCE

But what has all this to do with the question of "non-interference with the internal affairs of another country" as provided for in the UN Charter? The answer is that the principle of non-interference has already been violated in Kosovo on "humanitarian grounds" and in Chechnya on "security grounds". In both instances the wars are proving to be a disaster from both economic and humanitarian points of view. Nevertheless there is a real problem here because what do you do when ethnic cleansing takes place, or where the government of a country violates all human rights and inflicts genocide as in Africa today? Surely, in these instances it is only right to interfere on humanitarian grounds. Here we come across the sacred principle of "Conditionality" because no country wants to be told that aid will be given only on conditions. But reality dictates that gross injustices and genocide cannot be allowed and consequently there must be a role for international intervention especially military sanctions. Even Britain under Denis Healey, the then the Chancellor of the Exchequer, was forced to accept the dictates of the IMF and World Bank when its finances looked like losing the confidence of Wall Street and the money centres of the world. (This does not mean that there is not an important role for a reformed

IMF or the World Bank, but that interference must be in accordance with justice and right reason, as outlined in Chapter 3 about Natural Law, and the Cotonou ACP-EC Partnership Agreement.)

The splendid work of many charities, such as Oxfam, has also failed to achieve their potential because they are forced to spend much of their valuable money on relief work **after** war, when what is wanted are well-conceived regional or sub-regional programmes **before** war begins. It also needs long-term aid regional aid **after** war. Without well-conceived regional plans, integrating all the main issues, especially co-operation and disarmament, it will be almost impossible to appeal to the hearts and minds of the people and encourage a change of government minds towards peace.

A large proportion of aid that is now given on compassionate grounds, without fair and just conditions, does little to remove the causes of war and may even lead to releasing more funds to wage war. The ideals that inspire compassion should be harnessed to give Britain a new role in leading the world. We have lost an empire but have not yet found a role that could inspire the world. A beginning has been made by offering to cancel Third World debts but much more needs to be done, such as cancelling Trident, a weapon costing Britain in excess of £1,000 million every year. Rhetoric about a Marshall Plan is not enough.

AN INTEGRATED HOLISTIC ANSWER

Clearly a more integrated and holistic approach is needed if aid and development programmes are to be effective. The piecemeal approach by hundreds of UN Agencies and Charities, each with its own agenda, is far from ideal and is often a waste of money leading to "aid fatigue" and the withdrawal of money by the general public and governments just at a time when public support is desperately needed to encourage more aid.

This is why the idea of Regional Peace and Development Programmes is so important. Only by planning integrated programmes regionally and sub-regionally within a global context is it possible to encourage co-operation between potential enemies and promote human rights, good governance, appropriate development and a process of disarmament as provided in a Code of

Conduct. (see separate chapter). Clearly this means a degree of conditionality but it must be within the spirit of the UN Charter, especially where law and order have broken down and tyranny reigns. This degree of conditionality can be limited by calling upon the states in the region **to conform to international standards already laid down over the past few years by a series of important Prime Ministers' conferences** from most, if not all, of the world's countries. The subjects covered were,
Food: the Habitat: Urban Policies: Human Rights: Women and children: Population: Poverty: Unemployment: and Social Exclusion.

Although these policies are not yet mandatory, they nevertheless laid down principles, objectives and moral imperatives that could provide a yardstick by which to judge another country's behaviour. These conferences are planned to continue into the future and must be carefully monitored.

Another set of international standards (see Appendix) was agreed at the important Hague Conference of Non Governmental Organisations in 1999 and could have similar moral force. These guide lines should be made part of an agreement for any region willing to accept the disciplines of peace, development and international law in exchange for generous aid. The incentive to accept them would come from the knowledge that large scale aid in GRANT FORM, would be available over a 5-10 year period, adequate to jump-start the region into a process of permanent sustainable development. The cost to the rich world would be negligible compared to the expenditure on defence, or war that usually sows the seed for further conflict. In addition, by creating regions of peace and stability, based on co-operation and a process of disarmament, the regions themselves would generate internal investment. Private investment from abroad should also be encouraged provided it was given within well-conceived Regional Peace and Development Programmes.

5.9 THE MARSHALL PLAN

The Marshall Plan must be the example to follow. This imaginative plan was financed unilaterally by the USA after the Second World War when 2%- 3% of the USA's GNP, was given in GRANT FORM over a three year period to Western Europe on the understanding that the European countries co-operated and formulated their own economic recovery with help from the US (see Marshall's remarkable speech initiating the Marshall Plan in the Appendix). Why, cannot something similar be adopted today under UN auspices? Part of the reason the US supported the Marshall Plan was probably its fear of Communism, but despite the mixed motives, the Marshall Plan proved to be the saviour of Europe and turned long-term enemies into friends. The urgent need today is to have a similar vision and courage to announce that generous aid would be given to any region or sub-region in urgent need providing they accept the principles outlined in a Code of Conduct. Acceptance of regional cross-border co-operation by the poor countries should, however, be voluntary, but encouraged by the incentive of UN aid to ensure their co-operation and enable the region to feel that it is their own plan – an idea stressed in Marshall's speech. Regional Peace and Development Programmes should also be made available to those regions facing insoluble economic and ethnic problems. These aid programmes could be asked for from a new UN Agency in much the same way as requests for aid are now made to the World Bank or IMF. **The Proposal before the UN from The Commission on Global Governance to make the Social and Economic Council the engine for future development, equal to the Security Council must also be welcomed as an essential reform of the UN.** To avoid the accusation that "throwing money at the problem is not the answer, a Code of Conduct is essential to ensure good governance and avoid corruption.

The idea of cross-border regional economic co-operation, spurred on by outside financial help, has already proved its value in resolving the Irish Problem. The offer of generous cross-border financial assistance from the US, the EC and the British government must have played an important, but unsung, element in providing the incentive for the IRA and the Loyalists to co-operate and sign the Good Friday Agreement. In regions where governance and the rule of law have broken down, as in Africa, however, the incentive of a regional, or sub-regional Development Programme, together with a civil non-violent peace/police force, and a UN peace force with its transport and know-how for dealing with reconstruction and development, may also be necessary. These three strands of peace keeping/making would all combine to encourage conciliation and reconciliation

5.10 A CIVIL NON-VIOLENT PEACE FORCE

To help and encourage this process a UN Non-Violent Peace Force as proposed by the Fellowship of Reconciliation, (a pacifist inter-denominational organisation) and endorsed by The Hague conference of Non-governmental Organisations in 1999 should also be made available. So should the ideas of Brigadier Harbottle in his book PROPER SOLDIERING. At present the army is the only well equipped body able to go at short notice to a devastated area to bring quick relief, food and tents, and to restore communications, electricity and water supplies. It should also be trained in the techniques of reconciliation and conciliation. Brigadier Harbottle believes that a well-trained army as in Cyprus (where he was a former Chief of Staff of the UN Peacekeeping Force) can perform wonders, providing it is disciplined in non-violent techniques and is also part of a political cross-border solution. The following is therefore proposed consisting of:

1. A non-violent civil peace force;
2. The use of the world's armies for transport and reconstruction etc.;
3. Regional initiatives based on Marshall Plan principle
4. A UN radio/TV network to provide both sides in conflict with accurate information about the potential peaceful resolution.

These four proposals should be seen as complimentary and considered as an integrated whole.

5.11 SELF-SUFFICIENCY AND PUBLIC CONTROL

To conclude, it may be worth recalling the importance of the New Deal that President Roosevelt initiated in the US during the 1930's world depression, which saved the US economy and made it possible in 1946 to finance the Marshall Plan – the most generous and visionary plan the world has ever seen based on self-sufficiency. A similar plan, based on self-sufficiency, and helped by international financiers, was also one of the foundations upon which Hitler rejuvenated the German economy in a matter of a few years Of course we do not want to emulate Hitler's motives of aggression but these two examples of self-sufficiency illustrate how a measure of public control within capitalism (as proposed by Keynes) and the inter-play of economic forces, both national and international, can release the energy and potential of a state. The internationally known green economist Hazel Henderson, in her book, BEYOND GLOBALIZATION, also brings the idea of self-sufficiency to the fore by encouraging countries to set their own domestic rules and financial institutions according to their own cultures and domestic concerns. She illustrates this idea by saying that "the bounce back of the economies of Korea, Malaysia, Thailand and the Philippines, which flouted IMF advice, was the result of Keynesian deficit-spending to "stimulate their economies".

5.12 CONCLUSION

Regional Peace and Development Programmes could all be made possible if there was a UN Peace and Development Fund to finance them within a global context. A degree of control to regulate the present free financial market is also essential under the United Nations auspices. All countries also need to have free and fair access to the raw materials of the world. The World Trade Organisation should make this ideal possible, charged with the task of protecting the weak from the strong, based on justice and fairness. Safeguards must be made to avoid corruption and ensure good governance, as provided for in the proposed in the chapter Code of Conduct.

The above examples illustrate the urgent need for fundamental change from unregulated free trade dictated by powerful interests, to a world order based on regional and sub-regional approaches based on non-violence, self-sufficiency, and permanency principles.

6 Education for Life.

> Where is the wisdom we have lost in the knowledge?
>
> from T.S. Elliot, *The Rock*.

Never before has so much knowledge and information been so freely available but because there is no guiding sense of direction or philosophy it is leading us into the unknown future with dire consequences to us all.

It is true that in the material sense we are accumulating riches beyond the dreams of past generations but alongside this prosperity there is a poverty of spirit threatening to undermine the soul of the nation. Short-termism for a quick profit is creating a threat to our physical and natural environment and to our basic needs for un-polluted water, pure air and organic food etc., forcing us to ask what shall it profit a man to gain the whole world but lose his health and soul?

6.1 RACE TO HELL

It is ironic that this race to hell has been paved by the best of intentions, initiated by the churches, in the monasteries and in missionary schools, all aiming to liberate and free us all from the bondage of poverty and ignorance in the belief that the good life would follow as a natural consequence. Unfortunately this belief has proved to be only partially true because mental illness and crime of all kinds are at record levels. The original message of love is lost in the scramble for material success. Ethical and moral values cannot easily find a place in modern education concerned primarily with material success at the price of the spiritual.

Not that the spiritual side of human nature is neglected because there are dozens, if not hundreds of voluntary and civil local authorities providing thousands of interesting part-time subjects and in all state schools religious education is also provided for. Yet still there remains an important gap in our education system, especially as it concerns the most important subject of all – peace and war.

Although war has been averted between the great powers during the past few years, it has been a precarious peace with more people being killed in the past century than in all history. Technology has also advanced so much that nuclear, or germ warfare, or environmental problems could end all civilisations, while advances in medicine and agriculture are a mixed blessing threatening us with long term consequences.

Instead of living in harmony with nature, science has sought to dominate nature for short-term gains, ignoring the long-term consequences affecting our spiritual and physical well being. Instead our understanding of science and reason should be guided by wisdom.

6.2 DEMOCRACY

Under our present form of Western democracy our political, and religious and other leaders of public opinion, feel they are compelled to adapt to the art of the possible, determined by the climate of opinion – a climate largely dictated by self-interests and encouraged by a market-led philosophy urged on by a popular press and TV appealing to the lowest common denominator based on short-term policies.

We are all caught-up in this dilemma and many people feel helpless to change the course of events with the result that apathy sets in. Our task is to change this climate of helplessness to one of meaning and purpose. Fortunately the time may be coming when necessity compels us to change our way of life from greed and selfishness to one of dealing with the causes of crime, ill health and war, instead of the symptoms. Attacking the causes of crime is the proclaimed intention of the New Labour government, but this ambitious aim is not being fulfilled through lack of vision, resources and time. There is a new outlook and goodwill by the New Labour government but it has not yet been translated into any radical change.

Peace studies, organic growing, holistic medicine and prison reform are now emerging as important subjects but they are denied adequate resources so urgently needed if they are to fulfil their potential.

6.3 CHANGING OUR PRIORITIES.

The answer to these dilemmas must be to encourage our politicians to change their priorities about education. At present the British government proclaims its priority to be "education, education and education" and consequently it is increasing its spending on our universities by many millions of pounds in the belief that gaining more degree passes will automatically lead to the good life. This dream is an illusion yet we continue educating more and more young people in the materialistic things of life, almost to the exclusion of moral and ethical values. Thanks to modern technology the country only needs a comparatively small number of highly trained experts to keep the wheels of commerce and industry turning. On the other hand we urgently need everyone, including university graduates, to be educated for life, especially concerning human relationships in the family, the local community and world affairs if the aim of a culture of peace and non-violence is to be achieved. We also need to understand the relationship between our social and economic environment and our need for meaning and a sense of purpose without which life can be a recipe for mental and physical health problems and increased violence. Our priorities must therefore reflect these realities by reducing the cost of higher academic education and spending more on vocational training and Education for Life, as is the practice in other European countries such as Germany and Switzerland, where both countries have very successful economies. A well-educated society should be one that is based on a culture of peace, non-violence and co-operation as proposed by the UN

General Assembly in 1999. We need to return to the Ancient Greek idea of Academia schools of Philosophy that gave the world so much by so few under the guidance of Aristotle and later the Roman philosopher Cicero.

6.4 EMPLOYMENT

We also need a policy for full employment based on meaningful work with a purpose. This means everyone sharing and contributing to the wealth of the nation in a purposeful manner, working for the good of all. But our educational methods, based primarily on examinations and competition, do not reflect the need for co-operation in society. This is a moral, spiritual, and ethical as well as an economic problem, and is reflected by the popularity and success of many, if not most, church schools.

Unfortunately, government policy because of its bureaucracy and other political constraints cannot easily include values, meaning and purpose in life in its educational system. An important beginning has been made by the introduction of Citizenship and Democracy into the curricula of the state schools, but these studies are being resisted by many head teachers, not because they do not believe in them, but because it would mean reducing time spent on more academic studies demanded by parents and government inspectors. Many people already recognise that league tables and the demand for good academic results are damaging the child's' natural instinct for understanding and the search for truth. Saturation point in the market place for those with degrees is also happening, whilst at the same time there is a growing shortage of workers with special vocational skills.

6.5 THE VOLUNTARY ORGANISATIONS

The task of dealing with Education for Life is therefore left primarily to the voluntary organisations who cannot possibly find the resources to deal with the crises on its own. Not so long ago The Adult School Union and the Sunday Schools and the churches filled this role but sadly these educational centres are dying. Our universities originally started with a search for understanding about the nature of God but that vision too has got lost in academic research. We blame our church leaders for failing to give a lead and the churches depend so much on the "man in the pew" who is fed on a diet of misinformation in the popular press, more concerned with sensationalism, sex and sport than accurate news and informed opinion. Even when the churches issue inspired messages they are ignored by the media and their influence is minimal or ignored. TV and radio are also forced to appeal to the lowest common denominator, 'dumbing down' programmes because of their reliance on advertising. The BBC is not immune to this pressure in the race for the highest ratings. The competitive society also destroys the spirit of community by compelling us to compete. This spirit of competition extends to international affairs under the guise of free-trade and globalisation. Because of all these trends we are becoming an ignorant society lacking an understanding about the essential spiritual and moral values of life. As T.S. Elliot says in the quote at the beginning of this essay, "where is the wisdom we have lost in the knowledge"? We must escape from this self-imposed straightjacket of economic and political constraints imposed on us by governments but elected by ourselves.

6.6 EDUCATION FOR LIFE

There are two practical suggestions which could be adopted. First, to recognise that Britain urgently needs to recognise the need for a change in our values, and that this change should be reflected in the way we spend our money on education. Certainly we need a large number of experts who are specialists in their academic field of interest, but everyone also needs to be educated for life in all its manifold aspects: such as parenting, philosophy, co-operation, music, dancing, home and world affairs, cooking, painting, and many other skills which are needed in the family and in our daily life. History, philosophy and world affairs must also be taught otherwise an individual may be very highly educated in a specialised subject but ignorant of the some of the most important everyday things of life, especially parenting and human relationships at every level of society from the home to world affairs. A good grounding in the above, and many similar subjects, is needed to enable us to live meaningful lives, and play a useful part in the community.

To make all this possible, without reducing the total cost of education, the number of university places could be reduced and the money saved devoted to helping the voluntary and civic organisations to support the idea of Education for Life where **everyone** would be eligible and encouraged to attend short residential vocational courses dealing with everyday issues, as discussed above, without examinations. Examinations have their place but they inevitably tend to destroy the spirit of enquiry, community and co-operation upon which the good society depends. A comparatively small switch of emphasis would make this possible.

In Denmark there are about 100 such schools seeking to create "a climate where culture is a reality". Most are residential, running courses of 4-8 months during the winter, and shorter courses of 1-2 weeks during the summer. Residential courses are preferred to enable a spirit of co-operation and community to be nurtured and caught. Learning to live with others is as important as any of the subjects taught, but in Britain today we are becoming a nation of individuals lacking in a feeling of community. The subjects in these Danish schools include:

> Literature, history, psychology, ecology, education, music, drama, sport, dance, art appreciation, pottery, dressmaking, drawing, cookery, and so on, while some schools specialise in ecology, international relations, nature, conservation, and environmental subjects.

Being residential establishments, they can take students from a wide catchment area, thus enabling students from all over the country to have a wide choice of schools and subjects.

This educational approach in Denmark is a direct consequence of the legal requirement upon which the Danish Folk-Schools rest. They are required by law to provide a general broadening of education and are expressly forbidden to compete with traditional specialist educational establishments. Nor are they allowed to award marks or grades or to provide specific vocational training. Their principal task is to educate their students for life – in other words to shed light on some of the basic questions concerning life for people in Denmark today, both as individuals and as members of society. These aims are in accord with one of the founder's (Kold) objectives that students must be stimulated before they can be educated.

Today there are over 400 Folk Schools for Life across the Nordic countries. It is a trend that should be encouraged in Britain and other countries around the world. There are already many voluntary organisations in Britain but all are in need of financial help to enable them to achieve their moral and ethical potential. A small switch of governmental resources from higher education to vocational and Education for Life studies could harness this goodwill and expertise. **What is wanted is a partnership between the government and the civil society.** A Quaker Study Centre at Woodbrooke, in Birmingham, for example, is already pioneering theology and other studies about peace and community, but its work is severely handicapped by lack of funds. Denmark offers us an example to emulate because in that country the state provides over Dkr 500 million of which 11% goes towards the buildings, 66% towards teacher's pay and 23% towards student grants. In Germany there are some 50 similar residential schools, in Holland 30 such institutions, while Denmark has over 100. No two schools are the same because each expresses its own individuality, but all start from the same point based on the idea of love as expressed by the founder Bishop Grundtvig in the 1800's and the philosopher Soren Kierkegaard. If something similar could be emulated in Britain it could revolutionise the culture of the country (see the official booklet, 'The Danish "Folkehojskole', free from the Danish Embassy). Ideally what is wanted is for every town in Britain to have similar small, short courses based on community Residential Educational Centres with Education for Life, as outlined in this article, as its central purpose. These schools could then concentrate on subjects that would interest young people and give them the skills, knowledge and understanding of what life is all about without the fear of exams.

Much can, however, be accomplished within our present state system by providing a broader, holistic range of subjects for older children, leaving specialisation until a year or two later. A promising start in this direction has been made by the Development Education Association (an umbrella body for 220 organisations) who provide teachers to visit schools to discuss World Development and associated subjects. The idea of Democracy is also on the agenda. Whether this work will be adequately funded by the government, and whether adequate time will be found in the curricula remains to be seen. Welcome noises by the government are being made but no real money is being provided. A similar situation to the DEA seems to be the rule for music.

Nevertheless this first step within the present school system must be encouraged and expanded, **alongside** short-term **small** residential centres where a sense of community and co-operation can be taught and caught, and where all the many aspects of life may be included without the worry of exams. But Education for Life must be well funded to make it attractive to well-qualified teachers.

The idea of Education for Life, inspired by the Danish model, has been with us for many years but has always foundered on being unable to find adequate space in an over crowded curriculum. Subjects, such as music, are even now being dropped and the proposal for Citizenship to be taught is being opposed for lack of time. Nor can most day schools provide the ideal conditions where a sense of community can grow naturally and organically. Nor are the exciting possibilities of religious studies being fully explored. Small residential short-term centres near each town in the countryside is what is needed. Perhaps something similar to the YHA with its community atmosphere could provide that alternative. They should also involve local civil voluntary societies, as in Denmark.

The work of the Development Education Association, and many other voluntary associated organisations such as United Nations Association, must be commended as an introduction to Education for Life within the present state structure of education. But their success, unfortunately, depends primarily on being invited by the school and the degree of financial support given to support the visiting teachers, largely dependent on contributions from the European Community, charity funding and the Department for International Development. The total inadequate income, according to its 2000 Annual Report is only £376,990, a sum quite inadequate compared to the sums spent on other forms of education and for the immensely important work it could perform.

The need for Education for Life, and a changed culture in our national life, is clearly seen to be necessary as such incidents as the killing of the headmaster by a gang of youths outside the school gates. Also by the behaviour of football hooligans and other young people in our town centre. Crime is also at a very high record level and our prisons are overcrowded.

All these examples illustrate the urgent need to deal with the causes of crime through education at a young age. This means a new universal moral code of behaviour and a "culture of peace and non-violence for children", as requested by the UN General Assembly in 1999. The Cambridge Village Colleges and Fircroft College in Birmingham, all inspired by the Danish model between the wars, were brave attempts to provide an alternative and should be resuscitated with financial aid from the government similar to that given in Denmark.

Today we are witnessing a proliferation of weekend courses by the voluntary organisations and pressure groups such as the Human Scale Education organisation, the Communities for a Greater Bristol, the Religious Education and Environment Programme (a consortium of voluntary organisations) the United Nations Association, and the Parent-Link organisation. The local authorities also provide a wealth of evening and day classes, but most, if not all these activities suffer from under funding and are consequently unable to provide a spirit of community and co-operation that can only be found in well-conceived residential centres, preferably in the countryside, so essential if we are attain the culture of peace and non-violence requested by the United Nations. If the experience of other countries is any guide, many voluntary organisations would be willing to co-operate with the government, providing most of the capital expenditure on education could be found.

All these organisations need financial assistance to help young people break free from the culture of violence, drugs, apathy and self-interest, to one of co-operation and community.

Ecological studies must also be made more freely available, similar to those provided by the Schumacher College and many other organisations. Youth organisations such as the Scouts and Guides and the Prince of Wales Trust also need more support. The old established Workers' Educational Association and the University of the Third Age should also be given further help. All young people should also have the opportunity of attending one of the Atlantic Colleges where world affairs are taught in their residential schools around the world. There are also several **International** Folk High Schools in Scandinavia based on the Danish "Folkehojskole" model and grants should be made available for attendance. The ideal suggested by the late Peter Manniche, a follower of Grundvic, for rural colleges in the Third World, based on Education for Life principles, should also be supported as an integral part of any World Development programme. (Unfortunately Peter Manniche died before his vision could be realised). All these organisations and ideals could with more government assistance revolutionise education and remove most of the causes of conflict and war.

Funds should also be made available similar to the grants given to the Arts Council, or those given by the Danish government to the Danish Folk Schools, where independent voluntary schools are given very generous help to enable them to provide **residential** education for about three to six months for young people before going to work or undertaking further education. It is no coincidence that the culture of the Scandinavian countries, which have the most Education for Life colleges and the highest standard of living, is so admirable.

6.7 THE MEDIA.

The government should also legislate for a new TV and Radio service devoted to Education for Life, financed, if necessary, by a levy on all the commercial stations. The principle of subsidised funding is already operating to finance the Open University, and subsidised funding operated for many years between ITV and Channel Four. A beginning has also been made by the Independent Broadcasting Trust, a voluntary charitable organisation specialising in making programmes on development and human rights for the media. This work should be expanded to include many other similar subjects with a channel of its own. With the prospect of many more TV stations in the near future, the means must be found to finance at least one of them about the many exciting issues associated with peace and non-violence. The potentialities of the UN also demand far more time on TV and radio. It is disturbing that so many young-and not so young-people have very little understanding about citizenship, non-violence and the UN.

The need for Education for Life has also been recognised by the Council of Europe in its booklet, "Learning for Life" and funds may be available from this source and from the European Community under its new European Voluntary Service for Young People. The Dutch MEP Maarten Von Traa has proposed a non-profit making TV and Radio station to publicise the work of the European Community" an idea that should be supported.

6.8 VALUES

Education and the importance of values are claimed by all political parties as part of their rhetoric, but these aspirations are lost in the race for higher academic qualifications for everyone, with the result that our educational system is failing to create a peaceful and cultural society. Crime and the culture of violence are consequently at an all time high and must be dealt with through Educating for Life. This task cannot be left to the state schools if only because their curricula is already too full and is based on the philosophy of competition. The British prime minister's call for dealing with the causes of crime must be implemented in co-operation with the civil society.

6.9 PAYING FOR EDUCATION FOR LIFE

To those who say the country cannot afford to pay for Education for Life the reply must be that we cannot afford not to find the money. The huge cost of financing the police, prisons, and a whole range of social services dealing with crime, for instance, is directly due to our failure to maintain a civilised society and is costing us **billions** of pounds as well as ruining many lives . Home insurance against burglary alone, (according to the Insurance Association), is also costing the nation many more billions of pounds. Education for Life would deal with the root causes of crime and unemployment in the most cost-effective manner possible.

The time has come for everyone interested in Education For Life to co-operate. Government and the civil organisations together could accomplish something that each alone cannot achieve. Already there are signs of change and recognition that education, as we know it, is failing, and is now reflected in small changes in government policies. But a far more radical change is needed if the challenges of today are to be met and overcome.

7 A Code of Conduct.

A Code of Conduct between the UN (or countries such as the EC, the Commonwealth, or the US) and the region being helped is essential to ensure success, and that the money is spent wisely in accordance with international agreements. The basis of a Code of Conduct has already been agreed at eight important Prime Ministers' conferences over the past decade. These Summit conferences were about:

Children	in New York:
The Earth	in Rio;
Human Rights	in Vienna;
Population and Development	in Cairo;
Advancement of Women	in Beijing;
Social Development	in Copenhagen;
Human Settlements	in Istanbul;
The Food Summit	in Rome.

These Summit meetings resulted in splendid Declarations by the prime ministers of the world but were largely ignored by the media and by the politicians when they arrived home. Nevertheless they provide important guidelines for the future where none existed before, and have on occasion formed the basis of international law.

These Declarations will be periodically reviewed when it is hoped they will be given the force of international law. For instance, a Second Rio Conference about the Environment is due to be reconvened in 2002 and preparations for it are now well advanced. It is to be hoped that similar conferences will follow, dealing with other subjects when binding legal agreements could be made.

But there is no need to wait until there is world-wide international agreement because Regional agreements could be made more quickly if incorporated within regional holistic integrated concepts suited to the particular circumstances of the region as part of a something for something, or quid pro quo agreement, about economic aid specifically designed to bring peace and prosperity to the region.

Economic aid cannot be given unconditionally but only in accordance with a region's own natural aspirations, and in accordance with international agreements. This arrangement would free the region from accepting the narrow dogma about free trade, as has happened all to often in the past under the IMF, the World Bank and the giant multinational firms' auspices. This is not to deny the need for The World Trade Organisation because the WTO is essential to ensure the poor regions of the world a fair share of trade

Several issues are identified as important for effective regional Codes of Conduct within a long-term Plan. They are:

> Good governance, good administration and a Regional Secretariat similar to that formed for Europe under Lord Franks in 1946, which helped to implement the Marshall Plan. There are many experts available today in the civic society who could be enrolled in this task.

> Agreement to adopt the UN Declaration of Human Rights, similar to the European Declaration, these to include the UN Social and Economic Rights in addition to Political Rights.

> Agreement about what is meant by 'development'. A bottom-up sustainable programme is suggested, based on permanent long-term programmes such as tree planting, rural and urban education, water supplies, and land reform. Each region will, however, have different needs according to its history, geography and industry; therefore each region will require a different

A Code of Conduct

plan. All regions, however, should know and agree to general principles before applying for help

Support of a process of reconciliation and conciliation and co-operation at all times between ethnic communities. Also the creation of Regional Courts of law in cases of dispute. A process of disarmament should also begin.

Acceptance of the principle that generous grant aid would be given only on the condition that the states and ethnic peoples of the region, co-operate and help to formulate their own Plan.

In return the region would be given generous grants, similar to the Marshall Aid (not loans that have to be repaid) over a period of five to ten years, in yearly instalments. If the spirit of the Code of Conduct is not adhered to then the UN (or whoever is providing the money), would have the right to stop the instalments.

Ideally the money should come from the proposed UN Social and Economic Security Council as suggested in the Report of the Commission on Global Governance, chaired by Sonny Ramphal and Ingvar Carlsson. This new Council would have at least the same status as the existing Security Council and would involve all the nations of the world. If this is not possible there is no reason why the British Commonwealth could not initiate Regional Plans on its own, for instance, for an African Great Lakes region, as an example. The World Bank and the IMF could have a supporting role at a later date, if necessary, in accordance with the original Bretton Woods Agreement and the Regional Plan

The Regional Plan must be kept flexible enough to enable and encourage Non-Governmental Organisations and international firms to play an important role but that role must be part of the regional plan to avoid overlapping and excessive bureaucracy and to ensure that the aims of the Regional Plan are observed.

The region could be as small as an island, such as Sri Lanka, or as large as the EC, the Balkans, or Central Africa. The criteria for deciding what size be a region should be would rest with the region itself, but the over-riding condition would be that the states, or ethnic people involved, agree to co-operate and formulate an agreed Development Programme based on a Code of Conduct.

Most areas of the world form themselves naturally into regions or sub-regions for geographical reasons. Eventually it is to be hoped that each would become part of a larger region under the auspices of an organisation corresponding to the Council of Europe and the Organisation on Security and Co-operation for Europe. (OSCE)

The experience gained in creating these two organisations, plus that from the new Cotonou Agreement (the new 2000 Lomé Agreement), between the EC and African, Caribbean and Pacific countries, (ACP countries), could prove invaluable in helping this work.

Care must be taken, however, to keep the Regional Plan as simple as possible to avoid delay. Too much detail could lead to excessive bureaucracy and undermine the whole concept.

8 Conclusion.

"It was the best of times, it was the worst of times. It was the age of wisdom, it was the age of foolishness…it was the season of darkness, it was the spring of hope."

These few words of Dickens in The Tale of Two Cities encapsulate my feelings about today's world. There is much darkness and yet at the same time there is a light that shines, pointing the way forward. In other words, it seems that the world is at the cross roads between peace, prosperity, war and environmental and social disaster.

There is so much wisdom, understanding and new thinking about human behaviour in many sciences and religious faiths that could release us from our fears about the future. We could be entering the spring of hope, or a season of darkness – the choice is ours.

8.1 NEW THINKING

New thinking is obvious in the UN where numerous conferences are taking place under the auspices of UNESCO, UN Agencies and the Council of Europe, and in the growing number of Non-Governmental Organisations, and Civil Societies which are now playing such an important force in world affairs. It is frustrating that so little real action seems to result from these meetings, but the hope must be that over a period of time reason and common sense will prevail and the knowledge and understanding gained will affect international behaviour. On the other hand, man's inherent selfishness and greed affects us all and encourages us to support, via the way we vote with our money and at elections, crimes of all kinds, helped by the popular press and a media that thrives on sensational news at the expense of good.

For example, the encouraging news of the new Lomé Agreement between the EC countries and the African, Caribbean and Pacific countries (the APC countries) has barely been mentioned in the press, yet it offers great potential for the future. The bombing of Yugoslavia occupied the headlines for weeks, but the work now going on, striving to reconstruct the region under a so called Marshall Plan gets very little publicity. Whether this plan will receive adequate resources to undertake the huge task before it remains to be seen. The same could be said for the good work being undertaken by the UN Refugees and Food agencies who between them have saved many millions of lives. Europe (including Russia) is also at the cross roads, not knowing whether to seek a wider more loose confederation, such as a Europe of many regions, or a deeper unified large European Community, similar to the US.

The Middle East with its Arab/ Israeli wars, and Africa with its poverty, aids and environmental problems, threaten to explode, but who hears about the quiet research that is going on in the peace centres around the world striving to find the answers? The same could be said about our environmental problems. We have months of news about Mad Cow Disease and many other disasters but little publicity until recently about the organic movement. Even now, the research that is going into seeking the real causes of disease and conflict is minuscule compared to the challenge they pose.

8.2 RACE AGAINST TIME

There is a wealth of understanding to be unearthed about the meaning of life and how it can be enhanced, but short-termism prevents us devoting the resources needed. Trillions of dollars are spent on short-term solutions for short-term profits but comparatively little on the long-term well being of society or world peace.

Fortunately, with disaster staring us in the face, necessity is demanding a change and slowly, almost imperceptibly, things are moving. DDT and a whole range of pesticides and fungicides are now banned and even the possibility of banning nuclear weapons is on the agenda. The World Court has already ruled that nuclear weapons are illegal and the idea of a UN International Criminal Court is now within sight of being realised. Regional Courts are already a reality. These many positive acts seldom receive the publicity they deserve, nor do the countless small acts of kindness and concern undertaken by hosts of volunteers in charity shops and community centres. Whilst there is much to be hopeful about there is also much about which to be concerned. It is a race against time.

Even the rich countries are living on the precipice as technological pace increases and the world becomes more and more vulnerable and fragile and on the brink of bringing civilisation, as we know it to an end; the recent petrol crisis demonstrated how easily this could happen. An interruption in our electricity supply by a terrorist, or a bug in the computer network could also throw our economy into chaos overnight without even the use of nuclear or bacterial warfare. Mental and physical illnesses, such as Aids and the threat of BSE are also increasing in the West; perhaps because of the life style we live, whilst the fear of a global warming hangs over us all.

8.3 HOPEFUL SIGNS

As knowledge increases our fears grow: unless we change our way of life Armageddon may overtake us. On the other hand there are many hopeful signs, not the least being the realisation that war is no longer profitable, except for those engaged in the manufacture of armaments. No longer do our leaders go to war to find overseas markets, or colonies to exploit. Reality dictates that possession of colonies is seen as a liability – providing we can have free, or controlled access to the world's raw materials. The World Trade Organisation could play an important role here, controlling international trade for the benefit of the many instead of the few. Decentralisation of power and the localisation of the economy within a global context is the challenge of the day, if only for environmental reasons. This is a political and economic issue that cannot be resolved by war.

8.4 WAR IS OUTMODED

This change in our perception about the need for overseas possessions is a quiet revolution that has gone unnoticed yet the change should have a profound influence on our attitude towards defence and war; war is no longer a viable proposition as a means of defending our interests. Why waste money on defence when the fear of invasion is now minimal or non-existent – at least as far as Britain is concerned? The fear today is more one of internal conflict caused by social, ethnic and economic conditions, resulting in revolutions by minorities demanding to have their freedom and independence. There is also the danger of economic domination by the US and the huge trans-national companies in a globalized economy.

The change demanded today is of a very different kind from that of the past, based on "preserving the peace" by the threat of war, or, as the US bases in Britain like to proclaim at their entrances, "Peace is our Business". True the armed services have a role to play as a disciplined force capable of helping in reconstruction and providing air lifts in times of disaster, but waging war is now outmoded, as the experience in Somalia, Vietnam, Afghanistan and many other places has demonstrated. Victorian gunboat diplomacy is no longer viable and invasion of Britain virtually impossible thanks to European co-operation. Even Hitler's mad attempt to dominate the world is unlikely to be repeated in today's changed conditions, and could be prevented on a global scale once we have established a sane economic world policy and the rule of law as discussed in this book. An All Party House of Commons Defence Committee confirms this belief in its Report (Guardian Oct 25th 2000) in which it questions whether NATO – the world's most powerful military block could fight a coercive war again.

8.5 PROBLEMS OF TODAY

The problems today are more economic, social and educational and must be dealt with primarily at this level. The fear is that the US is attempting to rule the world through economic power politics but even in the States, the home of the big multi-nationals, there are signs of change as peace research demonstrates that social stability is a pre-requisite for trade and profits. Even investments in the defence industry are now a dubious proposition as technology advances throwing overboard today's wonder weapons. Buying shares in many of the traditional defence industries is now a gamble as technology changes so fast. For instance, whenever the possibility of real peace hovers on the horizon, as happened with the ending of the Cold War, shares drop dramatically.

This is not to deny the need for intervention when there is genocide taking place, but this can only be resolved by the UN adopting a multi cultural/economic/social/educational revolution encouraged by well trained civil personnel, supported by an army trained in civil engineering, transport and a multitude of other tasks, other than killing.

8.6 A BALKAN TRAGEDY OR A WINDOW OF OPPORTUNITY

All this is well within our grasp, as the Marshall Plan demonstrated in 1946-9. The Balkans tragedy now provides us with another window of opportunity, which the EC under Chris Patten, the European Commissioner for Eastern Europe, is already striving to grasp when he is said to be working on what he calls a "Marshall Plan for the Balkans". Whether he has adequate funds at his disposal to make it successful, or has the vision to implement it as a **regional** co-operative concept remains to be seen. But at least the EC has set its face in the right direction. The tragedy is that the Balkan war could have been avoided if a Marshall Plan for the Balkans could have been initiated before the war. The realisation must soon dawn on people's consciousness around the world that it is mad to spend trillions of dollars on outdated defence contracts when, for a fraction of that same money, the social and economic conditions that make for war could be resolved and the foundations for a non-violent peaceful international law constructed, as discussed in the chapter about Natural Law.

8.7 PREVENTING DEADLY CONFLICT

Another body looking in the right direction, and confirming the above diagnosis, in the recent book PREVENTING DEADLY CONFLICT by the prestigious Carnegie Commission. Its conclusion is to encourage and undertake peace research based on non-violent methods. The United Nations has also issued many excellent proposals and peace research is now taking place in many countries of the world. We have yet to see the benefits of all this work but if "necessity is the mother of invention", the hope must be that sooner or later reason must prevail. The alternative of nuclear, biological, bacterial warfare or environmental disaster is too dreadful to contemplate.

8.8 EDUCATION FOR LIFE

Education of the general public must be the long-term answer. It will be a very slow process but with modern means of communication it is surprising how quickly things can change. Dictators in Russia, Iraq, Indonesia and elsewhere have been overthrown non-violently overnight when the day before it seemed impossible. No longer can education and decision making be confined to the few, and public opinion is now a force to be taken into consideration, as events in Yugoslavia and Indonesia have demonstrated. But Education for Life (as outlined in this book), based upon co-operation and living in accordance with the laws of Nature is a slow process, and the sooner we recognise that true education means learning what true civilisation means in our daily life the better. Again there are many signs of change because most people recognise that there is more to life than obtaining a degree for work. Far more important is learning about co-operation and democracy, family life, community, life skills and world affairs and especially about the United Nations and Regional co-operation.

Everything, however, depends on the values we hold and the corresponding willingness to devote our money and political will to finance well conceived Regional Peace and Development Programmes within a global context. Only regional concepts have

Conclusion

the capability of enabling all the many aspects of peace and security to be integrated to combine in creating a region of peace based on the rule of law.

9 Terrorism – A Postscript to September 11

Since September 11 events have transformed everything and made even clearer the road we must take. Do we take the road towards world disaster driven by feelings of revenge, hate and fear, an eye for an eye until we are all blind, or the road marked, "social and economic justice, understanding and reconciliation"? In other words do we take the road that directly or indirectly promotes the basis of international law and national security and removes the CAUSES of terrorism? Or do we go down the road leading to retaliation, injustice poverty and more war?

A radical move in the right direction has been made by Chancellor Gordon Brown in a brave important and ambitious speech in Washington (Guardian December 17 2001) in which he is reported as saying, "today the Chancellor will invoke the memory of the post-war Marshall Plan to bank-roll a doubling of aid for the poorest countries to $100 billion a year (£79 billion)...and that..." we must seize this moment to win the peace". Speaking at the same American Press Club Mr Brown also said that the Marshall Plan was "not an act of charity but a frank recognition that lasting world prosperity could only be based on trade, development and freedom."

A similar speech, calling for a New World Order, was made at the 2001 Labour Party Conference by Prime minister Tony Blair. Both these speeches are very welcome but unless they are supported by an informed world public opinion they may remain a utopian dream.

Fortunately considerable progress has already been made towards changing this opinion. For instance, the International Peace Bureau, representing the major peace organizations of the

Terrorism – A Postscript to September 11

world in its International News Letter editorial of December 2001 called for a "Mega-Marshall Plan . Important peace organization in the US are also calling for the same idea.

The idea is already being partially implemented in the Balkans under the auspices of the OSCE, financed mainly by the EC. There is also talk of a Marshall Plan for Afghanistan and $3 billion dollars are being allocated for this work over the next three years (from 2002) with the hope of more to come. If this hope is fulfilled it would be important step to implementing a new concept of the old idea of Natural Law, and co-operation, as discussed in chapter 4; but the money allocated is peanuts compared to that devoted to the arms race.

Chancellor Gordon Brown has given the lead, but even with the support of the Prime Minister, Britain cannot go it alone and must have the support of other countries, especially the US. Regretfully the US Bush government seems determined to drag its feet and undermine development programmes by announcing a staggering $1 billion dollars DAILY increase in defence spending from a base that already far exceeds all other countries. To add insult to injury, especially to the poor world, the US is seeking (according to a Guardian editorial of January 25 02) to delete all reference from the draft target of the UN 2002 conference in Monterey, to the goal of implementing the UN target of 0.7 % of gross national income, despite the fact that the US gives less of its GNP than most, if not all other rich countries. This policy must inevitably encourage more terrorism and do nothing to remove the causes. We are clearly at the cross roads.

Perhaps encouraged by Gordon Brown's lead for World Development, the UN Secretary-General Kofi Annan addressing the World Economic Forum in New York on February 4 2002 made a similar impassioned speech saying,

> "we need at least an extra $50 billion of official development assistance each year if we are to reach the Millennium goals, including the halving of extreme poverty in the world by 2015. to which the world`s governments have committed themselves. That means a doubling of the present figure for ODA I see no good reason why the Monterey Conference should not adopt that extra $50 billion as an immediate, short-term target, to be achieved within two or three years."

Unfortunately, the President of the US, Mr George Bush, announced, (almost, it would seem, as a deliberate attempt to undermine Kofi Annan's speech) in his State of the Union message, that the US intended to increase its defence spending by a staggering $50 billion dollars. It also was made known later (Guardian editorial 25 January) that the US is opposed to implementing the UN target of 0.7% of each countries GNP and wanted "all references to such goals" deleted from the forthcoming UN conference in Monterey.

Instead of inspiring the world, as in 1947, when the US unilaterally gave Europe the most imaginative and generous aid programme the world has ever seen, the US is now closing in on itself and adopting an isolationist policy, almost certain to encourage more terrorism. Let us hope that after the trauma of September 11 second thoughts will prevail and world, and enlightened opinion in the US, will influence a change But why wait for the US to change; the rest of the world could go it alone.

To encourage this process towards global development, as envisaged by Gordon Brown and the UN Secretary General, the UN Social and Economic Council should be given the same status and authority as the Security Council, as proposed by the prestigious Commission on Global Governance in 1995. A global, or Mega-Marshall Plan, would make this UN Reform even more necessary. Well-conceived Regional Peace and Development Programmes must, however, include the concept of cooperation within a Code of Conduct (see chapter 7) to ensure good governance and to make the UN the primary engine for peace and security.

We are clearly at the cross-roads and must decide which road to take. It is often said that we have lost an empire but have not yet found a new role; We now have the opportunity to grasp that new role to find peace, prosperity and security. Mans extremity may be God's opportunity.

10 Appendix A: The Hague Agenda for Peace and Justice.

The Hague Agenda for Peace and Justice in the 21st Century emerged from a consultation in 1999 between seventy-two Organising and Co-ordinating Committees and hundreds of organisations and individuals from around the world. It was therefore an historic conference of Civil Organisations.

The Agenda represents what these Civil Society organisations and citizens consider to be some of the most important challenges facing humankind and should therefore be seen as representing world opinion.

The Agenda also provides valuable guide-lines for future regional peace and development programmes. It reflects four major strands. Below are headings only: the full text can be found in UN Document: Ref. A/54/98.

10.1 ROOT CAUSES OF WAR/CULTURE OF PEACE.

Educate for Peace, Human Rights and Democracy.

Counter the Adverse Effects of Globalisation.

Advance the sustainable and equitable use of Environmental Resources.

Eradicate Colonialism and Neo-colonialism

Eliminate Racial, Ethnic, Religious and Gender Intolerance

Promote Gender Justice.

Protect and respect Children and Youth.

Promote International Democracy and Just Global Governance

Proclaim Active Non-Violence.

Eliminate Communal Violence at the Local Level

Enlist World Religions in Transforming the Culture of Violence into a Culture of Peace and Justice.

10.2 INTERNATIONAL HUMANITARIAN AND HUMAN RIGHTS LAW AND INSTITUTIONS

Advance the Global Campaign for the Establishment of the International Criminal Court.

Encourage Close Co-operation Between Converging Fields of International Humanitarian and Human Rights Law.

Reinforce Support for the International Criminal Tribunals

Enforce Universal Jurisdiction for Universal Crimes:

Build Upon the Pinochet Precedent

Reform and Expand the Role of the International Court Justice in the context of a more comprehensive System of Global Justice

Strengthen Protection of, and Provide Reparation for, the Victims of Armed Conflict

End Violence Against Women in Times of Armed Conflict

Stop the Use of Child Soldiers.

Help Victims to hold Abusers Accountable under International Humanitarian and Human Rights Law

Protect Human Rights Defenders, Humanitarian Workers and Whistleblowers.

Train Grassroots Organisations to Use National, Regional and International Mechanisms in the Enforcement of International Law.

Promote Increased Public Knowledge, Teaching and Understanding of International Humanitarian and Human Rights Law.

Integrate Human Rights Protection, Resolution and Post-

Conflict Reconstruction

Build Upon the Successes and Failures of Truth Commissions and Political Amnesties

Establish a Universal and Effective System of Habeas Corpus

Subject War making to Democratic Controls

10.3 PREVENTION, RESOLUTION AND TRANSFORMATION OF VIOLENT CONFLICT

Strengthen Local Capacities

Strengthen the United Nations Capacity to Maintain Peace

Prioritise Early Warning and Early Response

Promote the Training of Civilian Peace Professionals

Refine the Use of Sanctions

Strengthen Mechanisms for Humanitarian Intervention

Engender Peace Building

Empower Young People

Support Unrepresented People's Right to Self-Determination

Strengthen Coalition-Building Between Civil Society Organisations

Strengthen Regional and Sub-Regional Capacities for Peace

Mainstream Multi-Track Diplomacy

Utilise the Media as a Proactive Tool for Peace building.

Promote the Conflict Impact Assessment of Policies

10.4 DISARMAMENT AND HUMAN SECURITY AGENDA

Implement a Global Action Plan to Prevent War

Demilitarise the Global Economy by Reducing Military Budgets and Shifting Resources Toward Human Security Programmes

Negotiate and Ratify an International Treaty to Eliminate Nuclear Weapons

Prevent Proliferation and Use of Conventional Weapons Including Light Weapons, Small Arms and Guns and Safeguard Personal Security

Ratify and Implement the Landmine Ban Treaty

Prevent the Development and Use of New Weapons and New Military Technologies, including a Ban on Depleted Uranium and the Deployment of Weapons in Space

Encourage Universal Adherence to and Implementation of the Biological Weapons Convention and the Chemical Weapons Convention

Hold States and Corporations Accountable for the Impact of Military Production, Testing and the Use on the Environment and Health

Build a Civil Society Movement for the Abolition of War

11 Appendix B: Marshall Plan.

SECRETARY OF STATE GEORGE MARSHALL'S ADDRESS INITIATING THE MARSHALL PLAN AT HARVARD UNIVERSITY JUNE 5 1947

The following extract is taken from the book FROM MARSHALL PLAN TO GLOBAL INTERDEPENDENCE, published by the Organisation for Economic Co-operation and Development (OECD) pages 228-229 to mark the 30th Anniversary of the Marshall Plan.

> "It is logical that the United States should do whatever it is able to do to assist in the return to normal economic health in the world without which there can be no political stability and no assured peace. Our policy is not directed against any country or doctrine but against hunger, poverty, desperation and chaos. Its purpose should be the revival of a working economy in the world so as to permit the emergence of political and social conditions in which free institutions can exist. Such assistance, I am convinced, must not be on a piecemeal basis Any assistance that this Government may render in the future should provide a cure rather than a mere palliative."

> "It is already evident that, before the United States Government can proceed much further in its efforts to alleviate the situation and help start the European world on its way to recovery, there must be some agreement among the countries of Europe as to the requirements of the situation and the part those countries themselves will take in order to give proper effect to whatever action might be undertaken by this government. It would be neither fitting or efficacious for this Government to undertake to draw up unilaterally a Program designed to place Europe on its feet economically. That is the business

of the Europeans. The initiative, I think, must come from Europe. The role of this country should consist of friendly aid in the drafting of a European program and of later support of such a program so far as it may be practical for us to do so. The program should be a joint one, agreed to by a number, if not all European nations".

12 Appendix C: Film on CD ROM – Peace Through Law.

This film now on a CD Rom was made as an introduction to small discussion groups, ideally in the home, together with the reading of NURTURING THE NATURAL LAWS OF PEACE, because without law there can be no peace.

But what kind of law?

The film argues that law must be founded on social, economic, political justice, co-operation, and by nurturing the natural laws of peace as understood by international thinkers from the Greek philosophers to today.

Originally it was made as a short 14-minute 16mm film for an American amateur competition in 1965 where it shared the prize; later it was transferred to video. Although it cannot claim professional status the ideas it presents are as relevant today as they were over thirty five years ago being based on a symposium as outlined in the book I edited in 1963 called, "Alternatives to War and Violence", now out of print. A similar book was later printed called, Foundations of Peace and Freedom; a second edition is still available and is recommended as a source of information (see below for address).

The ideas in these books, and film were well before their time and some have already become a reality, particularly the ideas of self-government for Scotland and Wales and for an International Criminal Court. The ideas of conservation, environmental problems and the abolition of nuclear power are also discussed.

So, too, are the problems of combining unity with diversity within the UN and these are illustrated by an orchestra. The film ends with Dame Laura Knight's official war paintings of the Nuremburg Trial.

Copies of FOUNDATIONS OF PEACE AND FREEDOM, 400p Ed. Ted Dunn are still available the original 1978 price of £4.50.

The book A STEP BY STEP APPROACH TO WORLD PEACE-REGION BY REGION by Ted Dunn 119p is also available at the original 1988 price of £4.95.

Both books are post free from Ted Dunn at 77, Hungerdown Lane, Lawford, Manningtree, Essex CO11 2LX. Tel: 01206 230434 (in fact you are only paying for the postage!).

Index

Adam Curle, iii, 23
Addis Ababa, 11
Adult School Union, 98
Afghanistan, 1, 6, 26, 27, 32, 71, 114, 119
Age of Reason, 47
Aid, 39, 44, 46, 76, 78, 80, 85, 89, 90, 91, 92, 103, 108
Alfred Russell Wallace, 55
Alternatives to War and Violence, 127
Altruism, 42
America, 40
Arab and Jew, 85
Augustus, 63, 64
Balkans, 5, 6, 26, 88, 109, 115, 119
Bishop Grundvig, 29, 82
Boutros Boutros-Ghali, 29, 82
Bracton, 60, 63, 71
Bretton Woods, 87, 109
Brian Urquhart, xiii, 87
Bureaucracy, 41

Cambridge Village Colleges, 103
Carnegie Commission, 2, 33, 71, 72, 116
China, 27
Chris Patten, 26, 88, 115

Cicero, 57, 63, 64, 74, 75, 98
Citizenship, 63, 98, 102, 105
Clive Ponting, 53
Code of Conduct, 8, 31, 35, 36, 40, 41, 44, 54, 68, 83, 90, 92, 94, 107, 109, 120
Commission on Global Governance, 33, 37, 39, 45, 87, 92, 109, 120
Communications, 72, 76
Communism, 1, 39, 68, 92
Conditionality, 78, 89, 91
Conflict Research Society, 7, 24, 25
Contonou Agreement, 80
Co-operation, 3, 4, 29, 67, 68, 69
Council of Europe, 3, 24, 39, 68, 72, 105, 110, 111
Culture of Peace, 50, 72, 86, 97, 103, 121, 122

D. V. Cowen, 60
Dag Hammarskjold Foundation, 34, 87
Darwin, 55, 56
DDT, 18, 113
Defence, xiii, 1, 5, 19, 26, 38, 39, 53, 60, 72, 84, 85, 89, 91, 114, 115, 119, 120
Denmark, 81, 86, 100, 101, 102, 103

Denis Healey, 89
Disarmament, 2, 59
Disease, 28, 53
Education, xiii, 3, 9, 10, 21, 22, 23, 49, 59, 72, 73, 81, 82, 84, 86, 95, 96, 97, 98, 99, 100, 101, 102, 103, 104, 105, 106, 108, 116
Education for Life, 9, 22, 23, 59, 73, 81, 86, 95, 97, 98, 99, 100, 101, 102, 103, 104, 105, 106, 116
Einstein, 60
Enclosure Act, 80
Environment, 19, 49, 51, 59
Ethiopia, xiii, 11, 12, 17, 81
European Community, 3, 5, 67, 70, 102, 105, 112
European Convention of Human Rights, 39
Evolution, 56, 61, 62

Fellowship of Reconciliation, 21, 93
Ford Foundation, 87
Foundations of Peace and Freedom, 49, 64, 127
Free Trade, 78
Friends Ambulance Unit, 10

Gandhi, xiii, 8, 10, 11, 17, 19, 28, 59, 81, 87
General Assembly, 2, 4, 45, 72, 86, 98, 103
George Marshall, 41, 44, 125
George Soros, 42
God, 4, 12, 24, 25, 26, 27, 28, 29, 30, 34, 36, 47, 57
Gorbachev, 6, 25
governance, 3, 30, 31, 32, 36, 37, 40, 43, 54, 65, 66, 67, 68, 90, 92, 94, 108, 120
Governance, 34, 37, 39, 45, 67, 87, 92, 109, 120
Greenpeace, 53
Grundvic, 104

Habitat, 36, 91
Hague Agenda, 65, 121
Hazel Henderson, 94
Henry Bracton, 60
Highway Code, 51
History, 60, 64, 73, 84, 96, 99, 100, 108
Hitler, 39, 86, 94, 114
Hugo Grotius, 54
Human Rights, 6, 8, 22, 32, 36, 39, 43, 44, 62, 64, 65, 66, 67, 68, 89, 90, 91, 105, 107, 108, 121, 122
Human Scale Education, 103

International Court of Justice, 48, 65
International Criminal Court, 5, 8, 21, 23, 43, 60, 64, 67, 78, 87, 113, 122, 127
International Folk High Schools, 104
International Law, 8, 43, 68, 75, 83, 88, 91, 107, 115, 118
Iraq, 4, 7, 51, 85, 116
Irish Problem, 92

Japan, 43, 77, 81
Jesus, 11, 17, 19, 20, 50, 59, 62
Joseph Lister, 57
Juries, 52, 53
Justice, xi, xii, xiii, xviii, 47, 50, 51, 65, 67, 69, 118, 121

Index

Knowledge, 101, 111, 113
Kofi Annan, 29, 73, 119

Lady Eve Balfour, 17, 18
Land Settlement Association, 17
Law, 4, 47, 54, 55, 56
Laws of Nature, 18, 19
League of Nations, 66, 86
Life Force, 58, 61, 62
Lomé Agreement, 3, 30. 80, 110, 112
Lord Caradon, 28
Lord Franks, 46, 108
Lord Melchett, 53
Lord Scarman, 69
Love, 57, 59, 61, 62

Marshall Plan, xi, xvii, 5, 6, 7, 25, 26, 27, 30, 35, 39, 40, 41, 42, 44, 46, 62, 67, 68, 69, 88, 90, 92, 93, 108, 112, 115, 118, 119, 120, 125
Michael Harbottle, 69
Michael Randle, 53
Milan Panic, 5, 26
Milosevic, 2, 5, 6
Mind-Set Change, 87
Mussolini, 32

National Peace Council, 20
NATO, 2, 3, 5, 88, 114
Natural Justice, xiii, 35, 48, 51, 53
Natural Law, xi, xviii, 1, 4, 22, 23, 33, 39, 47, 48, 49, 50, 51, 52, 54, 55, 56, 57, 58, 60, 63, 64, 66, 67, 69, 72, 73, 74, 90, 115, 119
Natural Selection, 55
Nature, xvii, 4, 8, 9, 11, 18, 19, 20, 21, 31, 47, 48, 49, 50, 52, 54, 55, 56, 57, 58, 59, 61, 62, 63, 74, 96, 99, 100, 116
New Deal, 93
New Economic Foundation, 34, 88
New Labour, 40, 97
Newton, 48
NGO, 46, 67
Non-Governmental Organisations, 32, 36, 67, 68, 69, 93, 109, 111
Non-Violence, 122
North-South Centre, 39
Nuremberg Principles, 6, 43

Order, 36, 118
Organic, 17, 18
OSCE, 2, 3, 5, 7, 25, 39, 110, 119

Pantheism, 57, 59
Pat Arrowsmith, 53
Pax Roma, 63, 64
Peace Dividend, 1, 7, 26, 85
Peace Study Centre, 23
Peter Manniche, 22, 64, 104
Philosophy, xi, 95. 96, 98, 99
Poverty, 42, 43, 79, 83, 91
Precautionary Principle, 78
President Clinton, 88
Preventing Deadly Conflict, 29, 33, 116
Public Control, 93, 94
Putin of Russia, 89

Quakers, ix, 8, 21, 23, 24, 61

Race to Hell, 95
Reform the UN, 9, 61
Refugees, 112
Rousseau, 63

Russia, 5, 6, 7, 26, 88, 89, 112, 116

Satyagraha, 8, 10, 27, 28, 59
Schumacher, 22, 104
Sean Macbride, 22
Security Council, 32, 33, 35, 36, 39, 40, 41, 45, 67, 73, 78, 92, 109, 120
Self-Sufficiency, 81, 93
Sermon on the Mount, 10
Sir Albert Howard, 17, 18
Social and Economic Council, 33, 92, 120
Soil Association, 17, 18
Son of Star Wars, 5
Sonny Ramphal, 37, 109
Soviet Union, 7, 25
Spirit, 61, 62, 63
St Paul, 59, 63
Stoics, 47, 56
Student Peace Project, 22, 23

Teilhard de Chardin, 56
The Scarman Report, 69
The Security Council, 45
The World Court, 34, 51, 87
Third World Debt, 21, 41
Third World Debts, 41, 68, 80, 86, 90
Thomas Henry Huxley, 55
Thomas Hobbes, 55
Thomas Paine, 62

Tobin Tax, 42, 82, 83
Trident, 20, 53, 90
Truth, 43, 47, 48, 55, 59, 60, 61, 72, 78, 98, 123
Truth and Reconciliation Commission, 43, 78

UN Charter, 2, 32, 33, 35, 36, 77, 78, 86, 89, 91
UN Declaration of Human Rights, 65, 67, 108
UN General Assembly, 2, 4, 72, 97, 103
UNA, 7
US Institute for Peace, 88

Values, 105
Versailles Treaty, 39, 68
Vietnam, 1, 27, 32, 71, 114

William Blake, 34
Wonder, 61
Wordsworth, 63
World Bank, 4, 37, 40, 73, 78, 80, 87, 89, 90, 92, 108, 109
World Development Movement, 34
World Government, 66, 67
World Trade Organisation, 38, 77, 78, 87, 94, 108, 113

Yugoslavia, 4, 5, 7, 66, 112, 116